KET

COOKBOOK

AIR FRYER AND MULTIFUNCTION PRESSURE COOKER

BEEF, PORK AND LAMB

Tasty, Healthy and Delicious Air Fryer Recipes

Easily to Prepare at Home

Robin R. Anderson

CONTENTS

.

Introduction

I love the air fryer!

Air Fryer food is so succulent and easy!

And here's something else I love?

Delicious meat dinners! So why not combine the two?

It's so quick and easy and everything that comes out tastes amazing.

I love it.

This is such a healthy way to cook meat or any other dish for that matter.

But with Air Fryer!!

Why?

Looking for meat dishes that steal the show?

Whether you need the perfect recipe for steak, chicken, or a slow cooked stew, we have meaty recipes for every occasion.

No matter what the season or the main dish, these meat recipes are for when you need to get dinner on the table... and you need it fast or when you have more time to cook.

This Air Fryer Steak is impeccably seared on the outside and tender juicy on the inside.

Cooking steak in an air fryer will create extra flavor and a delicate texture to truly satisfy everyone in your family!

Many health sources recommend air frying as an alternative cooking method for dieters hoping to eat the foods they love in a

healthier way; also,it is a great way to cook foods in a faster, for a healthier lifestyle.

The benefit to air frying is how much it shortens cooking time.

This makes the air fryer a no-brainer for a healthy lifestyle since these small appliances ensure fast cook times in dry heat.

And for me too, using the air fryer has actually altered the way that I eat.

This now book gives you many recipes for meat dishes that will help you get the most from your air fryer: from Simple Beef, Shallot and Turmeric to Bacon Crumbled Burgers, you'll be fueled and focused for the day ahead without sacrificing an ounce of flavor!

And remember, these are recipes that are to be savored and enjoyed.

What Is an Air Fryer?

The air fryer is essentially an amped-up countertop convection oven. (But there's a difference between air-frying and baking).

Nearly 40% of U.S. homes had one as of July 2020, according to the market research firm NPD Group.

Air fryers make it easy to whip up frozen foods, and they can do so in a way that is slightly healthier than deep-frying. The results are much better than oven-frying, and your kitchen stays cool.

The top reason for using an air fryer is so you can cook using less fat and oil: in fact you get the same crunchy texture you want with traditional fried foods, but with a fraction of the calories.

You can cook using less fat and oil.

Amazing right?

That happens because the circulating hot oil cooks the foods, keeping the inside tender and the outside nice and crisp.

All you need to do is get all the ingredients together for a recipe, pop them into the air fryer, and set the function, temperature, and timer.

Then wait until your meal is cooked to perfection.

Depending on what model air fryer you have, there are different features you can use.

How to prepare the air fryer and the ingredients

To prevent food from sticking to the basket, it is always necessary to spray cooking oil on the fryer basket.

Most of my recipes in this book use oil spray: I always use an oil spray bottle and usually fill it with avocado oil.

But you can use any oil you want.

Olive oil is ok too

Never crowd food in the air fryer or over-fill.

For some recipes, you'll need to turn the food around halfway through cooking so that it bakes and crisps thoroughly all the way through.

Finally, before cleaning it, first ensure that your air fryer is completely cool and unplugged.

All set?

Good!

Then let's get air frying!

Cooking with Multifunction Pressure Cooker

The purpose of this book is to give you great recipes that cover meal ideas throughout the day, for snacks and appetizer.

Multifunction Pressure Cooker transform the way you cook and make it easier for you to cook a delicious meal for you and your family as it combines the speed of a pressure cooker with the quick-crisping action of an air fryer

This appliance is a very friendly and easy-to-use kitchen unit.

Now, quick meals, made from real food and with great flavor and texture, can be on the table in no time.

And did I mention there is only one pot to clean?

Bon Appétit

BEEF, PORK and LAMB

Greek Beef Kebabs with Feta and Tzatziki Sauce

Prep time: 15 minutes | Cook time: 8 to 10 minutes | Serves 6

Ingredients:

- 1 pound (454 g) boneless sirloin steak, cut into 2-inch chunk ¼ cup avocado oil
- 2 teaspoons minced garlic 2 teaspoons dried oregano
- Sea salt and freshly ground black pepper, to taste
- 1 small red onion, cut into wedges
- ½ cup cherry tomatoes Tzatziki Sauce
- 4 ounces (113 g) feta cheese, crumbled

Directions:

➢ Place the steak in a shallow dish.

➢   In a blender, combine the avocado oil, garlic, oregano, and salt and pepper to taste. Blend until smooth, then pour over the steak. Cover the dish with plastic wrap and allow to marinate in the refrigerator for at least 4 hours or overnight.

➢   Thread the steak, onion, and cherry tomatoes onto 6 skewers, alternating as you go. (If using wooden skewers, first soak them in water for 30 minutes.)

➢   Set the air fryer to 400°F (204°C). Place the skewers in the basket and air fry for 5 minutes. Flip and cook for 3 to 5 minutes more.

➢   Transfer the kebabs to serving plates. Drizzle with Tzatziki Sauce and sprinkle with the crumbled feta cheese.

Per Serving

calories: 313 | fat: 23g | protein: 18g | carbs: 3g | net carbs: 2g | fiber: 1g

Prep time: 1 hour Cooking time: 40 minutes Serve: 4

Ingredients:

- 1 lb. beef stew meat
- 1/4 tsp. salt
- 1/8 tsp. turmeric
- 2 tbsp. olive oil
- 2 tbsp. shallots, sliced
- 1 tbsp. fresh ginger, grated
- 1 tbsp. garlic, chopped fine

- 3 cups of water
- 2 tsp. fish sauce
- 8 shallots, peeled and left whole
- 1/2 tsp. chili powder

Directions:

➤ Mix the beef, salt, and turmeric, use your fingers to massage the seasonings into the meat. Cover and refrigerate for 1 hour.

➤ Add the oil to the cooking pot and set to sauté on med-high.

➤ Add the sliced shallot and cook until golden brown, 6-8 minutes. Transfer to a bowl. Add the garlic and ginger to the pot and cook for 1 minute or until fragrant.

➤ Add the beef and cook until no pink shows, about 5-6 minutes. Stir in the water and sauce until combined.

➤ Add the lid and set to pressure cook on high. Set the timer for 20 minutes. When the timer goes off, use the manual release to remove the pressure.

➤ Set back to sauté on med-high and add the fried shallots, whole shallots, and chili powder. Cook, frequently stirring, until shallots are soft and the sauce has thickened about 10 minutes. Serve.

Per Serving

Calories 324 | Total Carb 5g | Total Fat 4g | Protein: 34 g

Prep time: 15 minutes | Cook time: 9 minutes | Serves 8

Ingredients:

- 2 pounds (907 g) ground beef
- 2 ½ teaspoons Taco Seasoning
- Sea salt and freshly ground black pepper, to taste
- Avocado oil spray
- 2 large ripe avocados, peeled and pits removed
- 1 ½ tablespoon freshly squeezed lime juice
- ½ teaspoon ground cumin
- 8 ounces (227 g) sliced bacon, cooked and crumbled
- ¼ cup chopped red onion

- 1 tablespoon minced garlic
- 1 canned chipotle chile in adobo sauce, seeded and chopped with sauce removed
- 1 small tomato, seeded and diced
- ¼ cup fresh cilantro, chopped
- Lettuce leaves or keto-friendly buns, for serving

Directions:

➢ In a large bowl, combine the ground beef and taco seasoning. Season with salt and pepper. Mix with your hands until well-combined. Form the mixture into 8 patties, making them thinner in the center for even cooking. Spray the patties with oil.

➢ Set the air fryer to 350°F (177°C). Working in batches if necessary, place the patties in the air fryer basket. Air fry the burgers for 5 minutes. Flip and air fry for 4 minutes more, until the patties are cooked through and an instant-read thermometer reads 160°F (71°C). Allow the burgers to rest for 5 minutes before serving.

➢ Meanwhile, mash the avocados in a medium bowl. Add the lime juice and cumin. Season with salt and pepper. Stir to combine. Gently stir in the bacon, onion, garlic, chipotle chile, tomato, and cilantro. Cover with plastic wrap, gently pressing it directly on the surface of the guacamole. Refrigerate until ready to serve.

➢ Top each burger with a dollop of guacamole and serve in lettuce wraps or on keto-friendly buns.

Per Serving

calories: 331 | fat: 28g | protein: 16g | carbs: 6g | net carbs: 3g | fiber: 3g

Creamy Ham, Bean and Butternut Soup

Prep time: 20 minutes Cooking time: 4 ½ hour Serve: 4

Ingredients:

- 2 tbsp. extra virgin olive oil
- 2 cups onion, chopped
- 3 bay leaves
- 2 stalks celery, chopped
- 4 cloves garlic, chopped fine
- 3 1/2 cups sugar pumpkin, cut into 1-inch pieces
- 1/2 lb. ham hock
- 8 cups chicken broth, low sodium
- 1 tomato, chopped
- 1/2 tsp. thyme
- 30 oz. cannellini beans, drained and rinsed
- 1/4 top pepper
- 4 Swiss chard leaves, rib removed and chopped

Directions:

➢ Add the oil to the cooking pot and set it to sauté on med-high heat.

➢ Add the onion and bay leaves and cook, frequently stirring, until onion starts to soften, about 2-3 minutes. Add celery and cook for 3 minutes. Add garlic and cook 1 minute more.

➤ Add pumpkin, broth, tomatoes, thyme, and ham hock, stir to mix. Add the lid and set it to slow cook on high. Cook for 4 hours or until ham if falling off the bone.

➤ Transfer ham hock to a plate to cool slightly. Stir the beans, pepper, and chard into the soup. Recover and let cook until chard is wilted.

➤ Take out the ham from the bone and slice it. Return it to the pot and continue cooking until heated through. Discard bay leaves before serving.

Per Serving

Calories: 324 | Total Carb | 5 g Total Fat: 4g | Protein: 34 g

Prep time: 20 minutes | Cook time: 24 to 27 minutes | Serves 10

Ingredients:

- 1½ tablespoon unsalted butter
- ½ medium onion, chopped
- 2 teaspoons minced garlic
- ½ pound (227 g) ground beef
- 2 teaspoons ground cumin
- 1 teaspoon smoked paprika
- ⅛ teaspoon cayenne pepper (more or less to taste)
- Sea salt and freshly ground black pepper, to taste
- ½ cup keto-friendly tomato sauce

- 1 recipe Fathead Pizza Dough
- ½ cup shredded sharp Cheddar cheese

Directions:

➢ Heat the butter over medium-high heat in a large skillet. Once the butter is melted and hot, add the onion and cook, stirring occasionally, for about 6 minutes or until soft. Stir in the garlic and sauté for 1 minute.

➢ Add the ground beef and cook, breaking the meat up with a spoon, until browned, about 5 minutes. Stir in the cumin, paprika, cayenne pepper, and salt and black pepper to taste, and cook for 2 minutes. Stir in the tomato sauce. Bring to a boil and then reduce the heat to a simmer. Cook for 3 minutes, then remove the skillet from the heat.

➢ Line a baking sheet with parchment paper.
➢ On another sheet of parchment paper, roll out the dough to about the size of your baking sheet. Use a 3½- or 3¾-inch round cookie cutter to cut the dough into rounds. Ball up the scraps, roll them out again, and cut more rounds until all the dough has been used.

➢ Transfer the rounds to a clean sheet of parchment paper. Place about ½ tablespoon of ground beef filling in the center of each round. Top with a sprinkle of Cheddar cheese. Fold the dough in half over the filling, using a fork to seal the edges together.

➤   Set the air fryer to 400°F (204°C). Working in batches if needed, place the empanadas in the air fryer basket in a single layer. Air fry for 7 to 10 minutes, until golden brown.

Per Serving

calories: 253 | fat: 21g | protein: 14g | carbs: 5g | net carbs: 3g | fiber: 2g

Steaks with Rosemary and Cheese Butter

Prep time: 15 minutes | Cook time: 10 minutes | Serves 6

Ingredients:

- ½ cup unsalted butter, at room temperature
- ½ cup crumbled blue cheese
- 2½ tablespoons finely chopped walnuts
- 1 tablespoon minced fresh rosemary
- 1 teaspoon minced garlic
- ¼ teaspoon cayenne pepper
- Sea salt and freshly ground black pepper, to taste
- 1½ pounds (680 g) New York strip steaks, at room temperature

Directions:

➤ In a medium bowl, combine the butter, blue cheese, walnuts, rosemary, garlic, and cayenne pepper and salt and black pepper to taste. Use clean hands to ensure that everything is well combined.

➤ Place the mixture on a sheet of parchment paper and form it into a log. Wrap it tightly in plastic wrap. Refrigerate for at least 2 hours or freeze for 30 minutes.

➤ Season the steaks generously with salt and pepper.

- ➤ Place the air fryer basket or grill pan in the air fryer. Set the air fryer to 400°F (204°C) and let it preheat for 5 minutes.

- ➤ Place the steaks in the basket in a single layer and air fry for 5 minutes. Flip the steaks, and cook for 5 minutes more, until an instant-read thermometer reads 120°F (49°C) for medium-rare (or as desired).

- ➤ Transfer the steaks to a plate. Cut the butter into pieces and place the desired amount on top of the steaks. Tent a piece of aluminum foil over the steaks and allow to sit for 10 minutes before serving.

- ➤ Store any remaining butter in a sealed container in the refrigerator for up to 2 weeks.

Per Serving

calories: 428 | fat: 36g | protein: 26g | carbs: 1g | net carbs: 1g | fiber: 0g

Yummy Mexican Pork Stir Fry

Prep time: 15 minutes Cooking time: 15 minutes Serve: 4

Ingredients:

- 12 oz. pork tenderloin
- 4 slices hickory bacon, chopped
- 1 chipotle chili, chopped
- 1 tbsp. olive oil
- 1 tsp. cumin
- 1 tsp. oregano
- 2 cloves garlic, chopped
- 1 red bell pepper, cut into strips
- 1 onion, halved and sliced thin
- 3 cups lettuce, chopped

Directions:

➤ Slice tenderloin in half lengthwise, and then cut crosswise thinly. Toss pork, bacon, and chipotle pieces together in a small bowl; set aside.

➤ Add oil, cumin, oregano, and garlic to the cooking pot. Set to sauté on med-high heat.

➤ Add bell pepper and onion and cook, stirring frequently, 3-4 minutes until tender-crisp. Transfer to a bowl.

- ➢ Add pork mixture to the pot and cook, frequently stirring, 3-4 minutes until bacon is crisp and pork is no longer pink.

- ➢ Return vegetables to the pot and cook until heated through. Serve over a bed of lettuce.

Per Serving

Calories: 312 |Total Carb: 5 g |Total Fat: 4g | Protein: 34 g

Sausage-Stuffed Peppers Italian Cheese

Prep time: 15 minutes | Cook time: 28 to 30 minutes | Serves 6

Ingredients:

- Avocado oil spray
- 8 ounces (227 g) Italian sausage, casings removed
- ½ cup chopped mushrooms
- ¼ cup diced onion
- 1 teaspoon Italian seasoning
- Sea salt and freshly ground black pepper, to taste
- 1 cup keto-friendly marinara sauce
- 3 bell peppers, halved and seeded
- 3 ounces (85 g) provolone cheese, shredded

Directions:

➢ Spray a large skillet with oil and place it over medium-high heat. Add the sausage and cook for 5 minutes, breaking up the meat with a wooden spoon.

➢ Add the mushrooms, onion, and Italian seasoning, and season with salt and pepper. Cook for 5 minutes more. Stir in the marinara sauce and cook until heated through.

➢ Scoop the sausage filling into the bell pepper halves.

➢ Set the air fryer to 350°F (177°C). Arrange the peppers in a single layer in the air fryer basket, working in batches if necessary. Air fry for 15 minutes.

➢ Top the stuffed peppers with the cheese and air fry for 3 to 5 minutes more, until the cheese is melted and the peppers are tender.

Per Serving

calories: 187 | fat: 12g | protein: 11g | carbs: 8g | net carbs: 6g | fiber: 2g

Air Fryer Bacon Wedge Salad

Prep time: 10 minutes | Cook time: 10 to 14 minutes | Serves 4

Ingredients:

- 8 ounces (227 g) bacon, sliced
- 1 head iceberg lettuce
- 6 ounces (170 g) blue cheese crumbles
- ½ cup pecans, chopped
- 8 cherry tomatoes, halved
- 1 recipe Blue Cheese Dressing

Directions:

➤ Set the air fryer to 400°F (204°C). Arrange the bacon strips in a single layer in the air fryer basket (some overlapping is okay because the bacon will shrink as it cooks, but work in batches if necessary). Air fry for 8 minutes.

➤ Flip the bacon and cook for 2 to 5 minutes more, until the bacon is crisp. The total cooking time will depend on the thickness of your bacon.

➤ Cut the iceberg lettuce into 8 wedges and place 2 wedges on each of 4 serving plates.

➤ Crumble the bacon and scatter it and the blue cheese

crumbles, chopped pecans, and cherry tomatoes over the lettuce.

➤ Spoon the desired amount of dressing onto each wedge so it drips down the sides.

Per Serving

calories: 910 | fat: 85g | protein: 27g | carbs: 12g | net carbs: 8g | fiber: 3g

Chef's Sausage and Spinach Calzones

Prep time: 20 minutes | Cook time: 18 to 24 minutes | Serves 4

- Avocado oil spray
- 5 ounces (142 g) Italian sausage, casings removed
- 1 teaspoon minced garlic
- 3 ounces (85 g) baby spinach, chopped
- ½ cup ricotta cheese
- ½ cup shredded Mozzarella cheese
- ¼ cup grated Parmesan cheese
- ½ teaspoon red pepper flakes
- Sea salt and freshly ground black pepper, to taste
- 1 recipe Fathead Pizza Dough
- Keto-friendly marinara sauce, for serving

Directions:

➢ Spray a skillet with oil and heat it over medium-high heat. Put the sausage in the skillet and cook for 5 minutes, breaking up the meat with a spoon. Add the garlic and spinach and cook until the spinach wilts, 2 to 3 minutes.

➤ Remove the skillet from the heat.

➤ Stir together the ricotta, Mozzarella, Parmesan, red pepper flakes, and the sausage-spinach mixture in a large bowl. Season with salt and pepper.

➤ Divide the pizza dough into 4 equal pieces and roll each into a 6-inch round. Spoon one-fourth of the filling onto the center of each round. Fold the dough over the filling and use the back of a fork to seal the edges closed.

➤ Set the air fryer to 325°F (163°C). Place the calzones in a single layer in the basket, working in batches if necessary. Air fry for 11 to 15 minutes, until golden brown. Serve warm with marinara sauce.

Per Serving

calories: 574 | fat: 46g | protein: 35g | carbs: 11g | net carbs: 6g | fiber: 5g

Tasty Bone-in Pork Chops

Prep time: 5 minutes | Cook time: 10 to 12 minutes | Serves 2

Ingredients:

- 1 pound (454 g) bone-in pork chops
- 1 tablespoon avocado oil
- 1 teaspoon smoked paprika
- ½ teaspoon onion powder
- ¼ teaspoon cayenne pepper
- Sea salt and freshly ground black pepper, to taste

Directions:

➢ Brush the pork chops with the avocado oil. In a small dish, mix together the smoked paprika, onion powder, cayenne pepper, and salt and black pepper to taste. Sprinkle the seasonings over both sides of the pork chops.

➢ Set the air fryer to 400°F (204°C). Place the chops in the air fryer basket in a single layer, working in batches if necessary. Air fry for 10 to 12 minutes, until an instant-read thermometer reads 145°F (63°C) at the chops' thickest point.

➢ Remove the chops from the air fryer and allow them to rest for 5 minutes before serving.

Per Serving

calories: 344 | fat: 21g | protein: 33g | carbs: 2g | net carbs: 2g |
fiber: 0g

Prep time: 20 minutes | Cook time: 28 to 32 minutes | Serves 6

Ingredients:

- Avocado oil spray
- 6 ounces (170 g) Italian sausage, casings removed
- ¼ cup diced onion
- 1 teaspoon minced garlic
- 1 teaspoon dried thyme
- Sea salt and freshly ground black pepper, to taste
- 2½ cups cauliflower rice

- 3 ounces (85 g) cream cheese
- 4 ounces (113 g) Cheddar cheese, shredded
- 1 large egg (organic or free range)
- ½ cup finely ground blanched almond flour
- ¼ cup finely grated Parmesan cheese Keto-friendly
- Marinara sauce, for serving

Directions:

➢ Spray a large skillet with oil and place it over medium-high heat. Once the skillet is hot, put the sausage in the skillet and cook for 7 minutes, breaking up the meat with the back of a spoon.

➢ Reduce the heat to medium and add the onion. Cook for 5 minutes, then add the garlic, thyme, and salt and pepper to taste. Cook for 1 minute more.

➢ Add the cauliflower rice and cream cheese to the skillet. Cook for 7 minutes, stirring frequently, until the cream cheese melts and the cauliflower is tender.

➢ Remove the skillet from the heat and stir in the Cheddar cheese. Using a cookie scoop, form the mixture into 1½-inch balls. Place the balls on a parchment paper-lined baking sheet. Freeze for 30 minutes.

➢ Place the egg in a shallow bowl and beat it with a fork. In a separate bowl, stir together the almond flour and Parmesan cheese.

➢ Dip the cauliflower balls into the egg, then coat them with the almond flour mixture, gently pressing the mixture to the balls to adhere.

➢ Set the air fryer to 400°F (204°C). Spray the cauliflower rice balls with oil, and arrange them in a single layer in the air fryer basket, working in batches if necessary. Air fry for 5 minutes. Flip the rice balls and spray them with more oil. Air fry for 3 to 7 minutes longer, until the balls are golden brown.

➢ Serve warm with marinara sauce.

Per Serving

calories: 292 | fat: 23g | protein: 15g | carbs: 6g | net carbs: 4g | fiber: 2g

Bacon-Wrapped Vegetable Kebabs

Prep time: 10 minutes | Cook time: 10 to 12 minutes | Serves 4

Ingredients:

- 4 ounces (113 g) mushrooms, sliced
- 1 small zucchini, sliced
- 12 grape tomatoes
- 4 ounces (113 g) sliced bacon, halved
- Avocado oil spray
- Sea salt and freshly ground black pepper, to taste
- Garlic Ranch Dressing, for serving

Directions:

➢ Stack 3 mushroom slices, 1 zucchini slice, and 1 grape tomato. Wrap a bacon strip around the vegetables and thread them onto a skewer.

➢ Repeat with the remaining vegetables and bacon. Spray with oil and sprinkle with salt and pepper.

➢ Set the air fryer to 400°F (204°C). Place the skewers in the air fryer basket in a single layer, working in batches if necessary, and air fry for 5 minutes.

➢ Flip the skewers and cook for 5 to 7 minutes more, until the bacon is crispy and the vegetables are tender.

➢ Serve with Garlic Ranch Dressing.

Per Serving

calories: 73 | fat: 4g | protein: 6g | carbs: 4g | net carbs: 3g | fiber: 1g

Prep time: 15 minutes | Cook time: 30 to 42 minutes | Serves 6

Ingredients:

- 1 recipe Fathead Pizza Dough

- 6 ounces (170 g) Italian sausage, casings removed

- ⅓ cup sugar-free marinara sauce

- 3 ounces (85 g) low-moisture Mozzarella cheese, shredded

- ½ small red onion, thinly sliced

- 3 tablespoons ricotta cheese

Directions:

➢ Divide the dough into 3 equal pieces. Working with one at a time, place a dough piece between 2 sheets of parchment paper and roll it into a 7-inch round. Place the dough in a cake pan or pizza pan.

➢ Set the air fryer to 375°F (191°C). Place the pan in the air fryer basket and air fry for 6 minutes. Repeat with the remaining dough rounds.

➢ While the crusts cook, place a medium skillet over medium-high heat. Once the skillet is hot, put the sausage in the skillet and cook, breaking it up with the back of a spoon, for 8 to 10 minutes, until the meat is browned and cooked through.

➢ Spread the marinara sauce on the pizza crusts. Top with the Mozzarella, cooked sausage, and onion slices. Dollop with the ricotta cheese.

➢ Set the air fryer to 375°F (191°C). Cooking one at a time, place the pizzas in the air fryer basket and air fry for 4 to 8 more minutes, until the cheese melts.

Per Serving

calories: 365 | fat: 29g | protein: 22g | carbs: 8g | net carbs: 5g | fiber: 3g

Quality Sausage and Pork Meatballs

Prep time: 15 minutes | Cook time: 8 to 12 minutes | Serves 8

Ingredients:

- 1 large egg (organic or free range)
- 1 teaspoon gelatin
- 1 pound (454 g) ground pork
- ½ pound (227 g) Italian sausage, casings removed,
- crumbled
- ⅓ cup Parmesan cheese
- ¼ cup finely diced onion 1 tablespoon tomato paste
- 1 teaspoon minced garlic 1 teaspoon dried oregano
- ¼ teaspoon red pepper flakes
- Sea salt and freshly ground black pepper, to taste
- Keto-friendly marinara sauce, for serving

Directions:

- ➤ Beat the egg in a small bowl and sprinkle with the gelatin. Allow to sit for 5 minutes.

- ➤ In a large bowl, combine the ground pork, sausage, Parmesan, onion, tomato paste, garlic, oregano, and red pepper flakes. Season with salt and black pepper.

- ➤ Stir the gelatin mixture, then add it to the other ingredients and, using clean hands, mix to ensure that everything is well combined. Form into 1½-inch round meatballs.

➤ Set the air fryer to 400°F (204°C). Place the meatballs in the air fryer basket in a single layer, cooking in batches as needed. Air fry for 5 minutes. Flip and cook for 3 to 7 minutes more, or until an instant-read thermometer reads 160°F (71°C).

Per Serving

calories: 254 | fat: 20g | protein: 17g | carbs: 1g | net carbs: 1g | fiber: 0g

Easily Sausage and Zucchini Lasagna

Prep time: 25 minutes | Cook time: 56 minutes | Serves 4

Ingredients:

- 1 zucchini Avocado oil spray
- 6 ounces (170 g) hot Italian sausage, casings removed
- 2 ounces (57 g) mushrooms, stemmed and sliced
- 1 teaspoon minced garlic
- 1 cup keto-friendly marinara sauce
- ¾ cup ricotta cheese
- 1 cup shredded fontina cheese, divided
- ½ cup finely grated Parmesan cheese
- Sea salt and freshly ground black pepper, to taste
- Fresh basil, for garnish

Directions:

➤ Cut the zucchini into long thin slices using a mandoline slicer or sharp knife. Spray both sides of the slices with oil.

➤ Place the slices in a single layer in the air fryer basket, working in batches if necessary. Set the air fryer to 325°F (163°C) and air fry for 4 to 6 minutes, until most of the moisture has been released from the zucchini.

- ➢ Place a large skillet over medium-high heat. Crumble the sausage into the hot skillet and cook for 6 minutes, breaking apart the meat with the back of a spoon. Remove the sausage from the skillet, leaving any fats that remain.

- ➢ Add the mushrooms to the skillet and cook for 10 minutes, until the liquid nearly evaporates. Add the garlic and cook for 1 minute more. Stir in the marinara and cook for 2 more minutes.

- ➢ In a medium bowl, combine the ricotta cheese, ½ cup of fontina cheese, Parmesan cheese, and salt and pepper to taste.

- ➢ Spread ¼ cup of the meat sauce in the bottom of a deep pan (or other pan that fits inside your air fryer). Top with half of the zucchini slices. Add half of the cheese mixture. Top the cheese with half of the remaining meat sauce.

- ➢ Layer the remaining zucchini over the meat sauce and top with the remaining cheese mixture. Top the lasagna with the remaining ½ cup of fontina cheese.

- ➢ Cover the lasagna with aluminum foil or parchment paper and place it in the air fryer. Bake for 25 minutes. Remove the foil and cook for 8 to 10 minutes more.

- ➢ Allow the lasagna to rest for 15 minutes before cutting and serving. Garnish with basil.

Per Serving

calories: 454 | fat: 31g | protein: 33g | carbs: 11g | net carbs: 9g | fiber: 2g

Spicy and Smoky Pork Tenderloin

Prep time: 5 minutes | Cook time: 19 to 22 minutes | Serves 6

Ingredients:

- 1½ pounds (680 g) pork tenderloin
- 1 tablespoon avocado oil
- 1 teaspoon chili powder
- 1 teaspoon smoked paprika
- 1 teaspoon garlic powder
- 1 teaspoon sea salt
- 1 teaspoon freshly ground black pepper

Directions:

- ➤ Pierce the tenderloin all over with a fork and rub the oil all over the meat.

- ➤ In a small dish, stir together the chili powder, smoked paprika, garlic powder, salt, and pepper.

- ➤ Rub the spice mixture all over the tenderloin.

- ➤ Set the air fryer to 400°F (204°C). Place the pork in the air fryer basket and air fry for 10 minutes. Flip the tenderloin and cook for 9 to 12 minutes more, until an instant-read thermometer reads at least 145°F (63°C).

➤ Allow the tenderloin to rest for 5 minutes, then slice and serve.

Per Serving

calories: 257 | fat: 12g | protein: 34g | carbs: 1g | net carbs: 1g | fiber: 0g

Prep time: 15 minutes | Cook time: 13 to 16 minutes | Serves 4

Ingredients:

- 2 tablespoons avocado oil
- 2 tablespoons freshly squeezed lime juice
- 1 pound (454 g) boneless pork shoulder
- 2 tablespoons Taco Seasoning
- ½ small head cabbage, cored and thinly sliced
- Sea salt and freshly ground black pepper, to taste
- 1 cup shredded Cheddar cheese
- ¼ cup diced red onion
- ¼ cup diced tomatoes
- 1 avocado, sliced
- 1 lime, cut into wedges

Directions:

➢ In a small dish, whisk together the avocado oil and lime juice.

➢ Pierce the pork all over with a fork and spread half of the oil mixture over it. Sprinkle with the taco seasoning and allow to sit at room temperature for 30 minutes.

➢ Place the cabbage in a large bowl and toss with the remaining oil mixture. Season with salt and pepper.

➢ Set the air fryer to 400°F (204°C).

➢ Place the pork in the air fryer basket and air fry for 13 to 16 minutes, until an instant-read thermometer reads 145°F (63°C).

➢ Allow the pork to rest for 10 minutes, then chop or shred the meat.

➢ Place the cabbage in serving bowls. Top each serving with some pork, Cheddar cheese, red onion, tomatoes, and avocado.

➢ Serve with lime wedges.

Per Serving

calories: 522 | fat: 41g | protein: 25g | carbs: 17g | net carbs: 10g | fiber: 7g

Tomato, Parmesan and Bacon Zoodles

Prep time: 10 minutes | Cook time: 15 to 22 minutes | Serves 2

Ingredients:

- 8 ounces (227 g) sliced bacon
- ½ cup grape tomatoes
- 1 large zucchini, spiralized
- ½ cup ricotta cheese
- ¼ cup heavy (whipping) cream
- ⅓ cup finely grated Parmesan cheese, plus more for serving
- Sea salt and freshly ground black pepper, to taste

Directions:

- Set the air fryer to 400°F (204°C). Arrange the bacon strips in a single layer in the air fryer basket—some overlapping is okay because the bacon will shrink, but cook in batches if needed. Air fry for 8 minutes.

- Flip the bacon strips and air fry for 2 to 5 minutes more, until the bacon is crisp. Remove the bacon from the air fryer.

- Put the tomatoes in the air fryer basket and air fry for 3 to 5 minutes, until they are just starting to burst. Remove the tomatoes from the air fryer.

- Put the zucchini noodles in the air fryer and air fry for 2 to 4 minutes, to the desired doneness.

➤ Meanwhile, combine the ricotta, heavy cream, and Parmesan in a saucepan over medium-low heat. Cook, stirring often, until warm and combined.

➤ Crumble the bacon. Place the zucchini, bacon, and tomatoes in a bowl.

➤ Toss with the ricotta sauce. Season with salt and pepper, and sprinkle with additional Parmesan.

Per Serving

calories: 536 | fat: 40g | protein: 35g | carbs: 11g | net carbs: 9g | fiber: 2g

Prep time: 15 minutes | Cook time: 6 to 8 minutes | Serves 4

Ingredients:

- 1¾ pounds (794 g) bone-in, center-cut loin pork chops
- Sea salt and freshly ground black pepper, to taste

- 6 ounces (170 g) cream cheese, at room temperature
- 4 ounces (113 g) sliced bacon, cooked and crumbled
- 4 ounces (113 g) Cheddar cheese, shredded
- 1 jalapeño, seeded and diced
- 1 teaspoon garlic powder

Directions:

➤ Cut a pocket into each pork chop, lengthwise along the side, making sure not to cut it all the way through. Season the outside of the chops with salt and pepper.

➤ In a small bowl, combine the cream cheese, bacon, Cheddar cheese, jalapeño, and garlic powder. Divide this mixture among the pork chops, stuffing it into the pocket of each chop.

➤ Set the air fryer to 400°F (204°C). Place the pork chops in the air fryer basket in a single layer, working in batches if necessary.

➤ Air fry for 3 minutes. Flip the chops and cook for 3 to 5 minutes more, until an instant-read thermometer reads 145°F (63°C).

➤ Allow the chops to rest for 5 minutes, then serve warm.

Per Serving

calories: 656 | fat: 40g | protein: 14g | carbs: 4g | net carbs: 3g | fiber: 1g

Prep time: 5 minutes | Cook time: 20 minutes | Serves 6

Ingredients:

- ¼ cup mayonnaise
- 2 tablespoons Dijon mustard
- ½ teaspoon dried thyme
- ¼ teaspoon dried rosemary
- 1 (1-pound / 454-g) pork tenderloin
- ½ teaspoon salt
- ¼ teaspoon ground black pepper

Directions:

➤ In a small bowl, mix mayonnaise, mustard, thyme, and rosemary. Brush tenderloin with mixture on all sides, then sprinkle with salt and pepper on all sides.

➤ Place tenderloin into ungreased air fryer basket. Adjust the temperature to 400°F (204°C) and air fry for 20 minutes, turning tenderloin halfway through cooking.

➤ Tenderloin will be golden and have an internal temperature of at least 145°F (63°C) when done. Serve warm.

Per Serving

calories: 158 | fat: 9g | protein: 16g | carbs: 1g | net carbs: 1g | fiber: 0g

Prep time: 5 minutes | Cook time: 12 minutes | Serves 4

Ingredients:

- 4 (4-ounce / 113-g) boneless pork chops
- ½ teaspoon salt
- ¼ teaspoon ground black pepper
- 2 tablespoons salted butter, softened

Directions:

➢ Sprinkle pork chops on all sides with salt and pepper. Place chops into ungreased air fryer basket in a single layer. Adjust the temperature to 400°F (204°C) and air fry for 12 minutes.

➢ Pork chops will be golden and have an internal temperature of at least 145°F (63°C) when done.

➢ Use tongs to remove cooked pork chops from air fryer and place onto a large plate. Top each chop with ½ tablespoon butter and let sit 2 minutes to melt. Serve warm.

Per Serving

calories: 78 | fat: 19g | protein: 24g | carbs: 0g | net carbs: 0g | fiber: 0g

Prep time: 10 minutes | Cook time: 12 minutes | Serves 4

Ingredients:

- ½ ounce (14 g) plain pork rinds, finely crushed
- ½ cup shredded sharp Cheddar cheese
- 4 slices cooked sugar-free bacon, crumbled
- 4 ounce (113-g) boneless pork chops
- ½ teaspoon salt
- ¼ teaspoon ground black pepper

Directions:

➤ In a small bowl, mix pork rinds, Cheddar, and bacon.

➤ Make a 3-inch slit in the side of each pork chop and stuff with ¼ pork rind mixture.

➤ Sprinkle each side of pork chops with salt and pepper.

➤ Place pork chops into ungreased air fryer basket, stuffed side up.

➤ Adjust the temperature to 400°F (204°C) and air fry for 12 minutes.

➤ Pork chops will be browned and have an internal temperature of at least 145°F (63°C) when done. Serve warm.

Per Serving

calories: 348 | fat: 22g | protein: 33g | carbs: 0g | net carbs: 0g | fiber: 0g

Parmesan cheese-Crusted Pork Chops

Prep time: 5 minutes | Cook time: 12 minutes | Serves 4

Ingredients:

- 1 large egg (organic or free range)
- ½ cup grated Parmesan cheese
- 4 (4-ounce / 113-g) boneless pork chops
- ½ teaspoon salt
- ¼ teaspoon ground black pepper

Directions:

➤ Whisk egg in a medium bowl and place Parmesan in a separate medium bowl.

➤ Sprinkle pork chops on both sides with salt and pepper. Dip each pork chop into egg, then press both sides into Parmesan.

➤ Place pork chops into ungreased air fryer basket. Adjust the temperature to 400°F (204°C) and air fry for 12 minutes, turning chops halfway through cooking.

➤ Pork chops will be golden and have an internal temperature of at least 145°F (63°C) when done. Serve warm.

Per Serving

calories: 298 | fat: 17g | protein: 29g | carbs: 2g | net carbs: 2g | fiber: 0g

Mustard Pork Spare Ribs

Prep time: 10 minutes | Cook time: 30 minutes | Serves 4

Ingredients:

- 1 (4-pound / 1.8-kg) rack pork spare ribs
- 1 teaspoon ground cumin
- 2 teaspoons salt
- 1 teaspoon ground black pepper
- 1 teaspoon garlic powder
- ½ teaspoon dry ground mustard
- ½ cup low-carb barbecue sauce

Directions:

- Place ribs on ungreased aluminum foil sheet.
- Carefully use a knife to remove membrane and sprinkle meat evenly on both sides with cumin, salt, pepper, garlic powder, and ground mustard.
- Cut rack into portions that will fit in your air fryer, and wrap each portion in one layer of aluminum foil, working in batches if needed.
- Place ribs into ungreased air fryer basket. Adjust the temperature to 400°F (204°C) and air fry for 25 minutes.

➢ Carefully remove ribs from foil and brush with barbecue sauce. Return to air fryer and cook at 400°F (204°C) for an additional 5 minutes to brown.

➢ Ribs will be done when no pink remains and internal temperature is at least 180°F (82°C). Serve warm.

Per Serving

calories: 192 | fat: 12g | protein: 13g | carbs: 3g | net carbs: 3g | fiber: 0g

Chipotle Sauce Shredded Beef

Prep time: 5 minutes | Cook time: 35 minutes | Serves 6

Ingredients:

- 1 (2-pound / 907-g) beef chuck roast, cut into 2-inch cubes
- 1 teaspoon salt
- ½ teaspoon ground black pepper
- ½ cup no-sugar-added chipotle sauce

Directions:

➤ In a large bowl, sprinkle beef cubes with salt and pepper and toss to coat. Place beef into ungreased air fryer basket.

➢ Adjust the temperature to 400°F (204°C) and air fry for 30 minutes, shaking the basket halfway through cooking. Beef will be done when internal temperature is at least 160°F (71°C).

➢ Place cooked beef into a large bowl and shred with two forks. Pour in chipotle sauce and toss to coat.

➢ Return beef to air fryer basket for an additional 5 minutes at 400°F (204°C) to crisp with sauce. Serve warm.

Per Serving

calories: 217 | fat: 6g | protein: 37g | carbs: 0g | net carbs: 0g | fiber: 0g

Pork Meatballs and Ginger

Prep time: 10 minutes | Cook time: 12 minutes | Makes 18 meatballs

Ingredients:

- 1 pound (454 g) ground pork
- 1 large egg (organic or free range), whisked
- ½ teaspoon garlic powder
- ½ teaspoon salt
- ½ teaspoon ground ginger
- ¼ teaspoon crushed red pepper flakes
- 1 medium scallion, trimmed and sliced

Directions:

➢ Combine all ingredients in a large bowl. Spoon out 2 tablespoons mixture and roll into a ball. Repeat to form eighteen meatballs total.

➢ Place meatballs into ungreased air fryer basket. Adjust the temperature to 400°F (204°C) and air fry for 12 minutes, shaking the basket three times throughout cooking.

➢ Meatballs will be browned and have an internal temperature of at least 145°F (63°C) when done. Serve warm.

Per Serving **(3 meatballs)**

calories: 164 | fat: 10g | protein: 15g | carbs: 1g | net carbs: 1g | fiber: 0g

Chili-Rubbed Pork Loin

Prep time: 5 minutes | Cook time: 20 minutes | Serves 6

Ingredients:

- 1 teaspoon paprika
- ½ teaspoon ground cumin
- ½ teaspoon chili powder
- ½ teaspoon garlic powder
- 2 tablespoons coconut oil
- 1 (1½-pound / 680-g) boneless pork loin
- ½ teaspoon salt
- ¼ teaspoon ground black pepper

Directions:

➢ In a small bowl, mix paprika, cumin, chili powder, and garlic powder. Drizzle coconut oil over pork. Sprinkle pork loin with salt and pepper, then rub spice mixture evenly on all sides.

➢ Place pork loin into ungreased air fryer basket. Adjust the temperature to 400°F (204°C) and air fry for 20 minutes, turning pork halfway through cooking. Pork loin will be browned and have an internal temperature of at least 145°F (63°C) when done. Serve warm.

Per Serving

calories: 249 | fat: 16g | protein: 24g | carbs: 1g | net carbs: 1g | fiber: 0g

Paprika Steak Nuggets

Prep time: 10 minutes | Cook time: 7 minutes | Serves 2

Ingredients:

- 1 pound (454 g) rib eye steak, cut into 1-inch cubes
- 2 tablespoons salted butter, melted
- ½ teaspoon paprika
- ½ teaspoon salt
- ¼ teaspoon garlic powder
- ¼ teaspoon onion powder
- ¼ teaspoon ground black pepper
- ⅛ teaspoon cayenne pepper

Directions:

➢ Place steak into a large bowl and pour in butter. Toss to coat. Sprinkle with remaining ingredients.

➢ Place bites into ungreased air fryer basket. Adjust the temperature to 400°F (204°C) and air fry for 7 minutes, shaking the basket three times during cooking.

➢ Steak will be crispy on the outside and browned when done and internal temperature is at least 150°F (66°C) for medium and 180°F (82°C) for well-done. Serve warm.

Per Serving

calories: 466 | fat: 28g | protein: 49g | carbs: 1g | net carbs: 1g | fiber: 0g

Quality Spinach and Provolone Steak Rolls

Prep time: 10 minutes | Cook time: 12 minutes | Makes 8 rolls

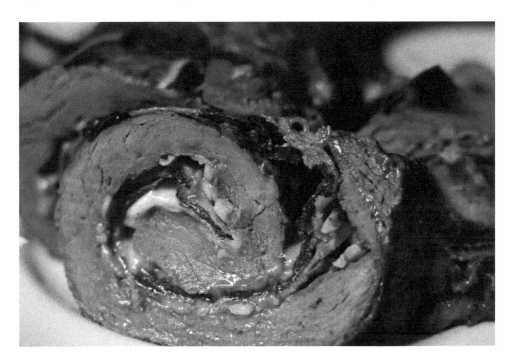

Ingredients:

- 1 pound (454-g) flank steak, butterflied
- 8 (1-ounce / 28-g, ¼-inch-thick) deli slices provolone
- cheese
- 1 cup fresh spinach leaves
- ½ teaspoon salt
- ¼ teaspoon ground black pepper

Directions:

- ➤ Place steak on a large plate. Place provolone slices to cover steak, leaving 1-inch at the edges.

- ➤ Lay spinach leaves over cheese.

- ➤ Gently roll steak and tie with kitchen twine or secure with toothpicks. Carefully slice into eight pieces.

- ➤ Sprinkle each with salt and pepper.

- ➤ Place rolls into ungreased air fryer basket, cut side up. Adjust the temperature to 400°F (204°C) and air fry for 12 minutes.

- ➤ Steak rolls will be browned and cheese will be melted when done and have an internal temperature of at least 150°F (66°C) for medium steak and 180°F (82°C) for well-done steak.

- ➤ Serve warm.

Per Serving (2 rolls)

calories: 376 | fat: 21g | protein: 40g | carbs: 2g | net carbs: 2g | fiber: 0g

Chorizo-Jalapeños and Beef Burger

Prep time: 10 minutes | Cook time: 15 minutes | Serves 4

Ingredients:

- ¾ pound (340 g) 80/20 ground beef
- ¼ pound (113 g) Mexican-style ground chorizo
- ¼ cup chopped onion
- 5 slices pickled jalapeños, chopped
- 2 teaspoons chili powder
- 1 teaspoon minced garlic
- ¼ teaspoon cumin

Directions:

➢ In a large bowl, mix all ingredients. Divide the mixture into four sections and form them into burger patties.

➢ Place burger patties into the air fryer basket, working in batches if necessary.

➢ Adjust the temperature to 375°F (191°C) and air fry for 15 minutes.

➢ Flip the patties halfway through the cooking time. Serve warm.

Per Serving

calories: 291 | fat: 18g | protein: 21g | carbs: 5g | net carbs: 4g | fiber: 1g

Baby Back Ribs with Barbecue Sauce

Prep time: 5 minutes | Cook time: 25 minutes | Serves 4

Ingredients:

- 2 pounds (907 g) baby back ribs
- 2 teaspoons chili powder
- 1 teaspoon paprika
- ½ teaspoon onion powder
- ½ teaspoon garlic powder
- ¼ teaspoon ground cayenne pepper
- ½ cup low-carb, sugar-free barbecue sauce

Directions:

➢ Rub ribs with all ingredients except barbecue sauce. Place into the air fryer basket.

➢ Adjust the temperature to 400°F (204°C) and roast for 25 minutes.

➢ When done, ribs will be dark and charred with an internal temperature of at least 185°F (85°C).

➢ Brush ribs with barbecue sauce and serve warm.

Per Serving

calories: 650 | fat: 51g | protein: 40g | carbs: 4g | net carbs: 3g | fiber: 1g

Pigs with Mozzarella Cheese

Prep time: 10 minutes | Cook time: 7 minutes | Serves 2

Ingredients:

- ½ cup shredded Mozzarella cheese
- 2 tablespoons blanched finely ground almond flour
- 1 ounce (28 g) full-fat cream cheese
- 2 (2-ounce / 57-g) beef smoked sausages
- ½ teaspoon sesame seeds

Directions:

➢ Place Mozzarella, almond flour, and cream cheese in a large microwave- safe bowl.

➢ Microwave for 45 seconds and stir until smooth.

➢ Roll dough into a ball and cut in half.

➢ Press each half out into a 4 × 5-inch rectangle.

➢ Roll one sausage up in each dough half and press seams closed.

➢ Sprinkle the top with sesame seeds.

➢ Place each wrapped sausage into the air fryer basket.

➢ Adjust the temperature to 400°F (204°C) and air fry for 7 minutes.

➢ The outside will be golden when completely cooked. Serve immediately.

Per Serving

calories: 405 | fat: 32g | protein: 17g | carbs: 3g | net carbs: 2g | fiber: 1g

Crispy Beef and Broccoli Stir-Fry

Prep time: 10 minutes | Cook time: 20 minutes | Serves 2

Ingredients:

- ½ pound (227 g) sirloin steak, thinly sliced
- 2 tablespoons coconut aminos
- ¼ teaspoon grated ginger
- ¼ teaspoon finely minced garlic
- 1 tablespoon coconut oil
- 2 cups broccoli florets
- ¼ teaspoon crushed red pepper
- ⅛ teaspoon xanthan gum
- ½ teaspoon sesame seeds

Directions:

➢ To marinate beef, place it into a large bowl or storage bag and add coconut aminos, ginger, garlic, and coconut oil.

➢ Allow to marinate for 1 hour in refrigerator.

➢ Remove beef from marinade, reserving marinade, and place beef into the air fryer basket.

➢ Adjust the temperature to 320°F (160°C) and air fry for 20 minutes.

➢ After 10 minutes, add broccoli and sprinkle red pepper into the fryer basket and shake.

- ➤ Pour the marinade into a skillet over medium heat and bring to a boil, then reduce to simmer.

- ➤ Stir in xanthan gum and allow to thicken.

- ➤ When done, quickly empty fryer basket into skillet and toss. Sprinkle with sesame seeds.

- ➤ Serve immediately.

Per Serving

calories: 342 | fat: 19g | protein: 27g | carbs: 10g | net carbs: 7g | fiber: 3g

Peppercorn-Crusted Beef Tenderloin

Prep time: 10 minutes | Cook time: 25 minutes | Serves 6

Ingredients:

- 2 tablespoons salted butter, melted
- 2 teaspoons minced roasted garlic
- 3 tablespoons ground
- 4-peppercorn blend
- 1 (2-pound / 907-g) beef tenderloin, trimmed of visible fat

Directions:

➢ In a small bowl, mix the butter and roasted garlic.

➢ Brush it over the beef tenderloin.

➢ Place the ground peppercorns onto a plate and roll the tenderloin through them, creating a crust.

➢ Place tenderloin into the air fryer basket.

➢ Adjust the temperature to 400°F (204°C) and roast for 25 minutes.

➢ Turn the tenderloin halfway through the cooking time.

➢ Allow meat to rest 10 minutes before slicing.

Per Serving

calories: 289 | fat: 14g | protein: 35g | carbs: 3g | net carbs: 2g | fiber: 1g

Prep time: 20 minutes | Cook time: 10 minutes | Serves 4

Ingredients:

- ½ pound (227 g) 80/20 ground beef
- ⅓ cup water
- 1 tablespoon chili powder
- 2 teaspoons cumin
- ½ teaspoon garlic powder
- ¼ teaspoon dried oregano
- ¼ cup canned diced tomatoes and chiles, drained
- 2 tablespoons chopped cilantro
- 1½ cups shredded Mozzarella cheese
- ½ cup blanched finely ground almond flour
- 2 ounces (57 g) full-fat cream cheese
- 1 large egg (organic or free range)

Directions:

In a medium skillet over medium heat, brown the ground beef about 7 to 10 minutes. When meat is fully cooked, drain.

- Add water to skillet and stir in chili powder, cumin, garlic powder, oregano, and tomatoes with chiles. Add cilantro. Bring to a boil, then reduce heat to simmer for 3 minutes.

- In a large microwave-safe bowl, place Mozzarella, almond flour, cream cheese, and egg. Microwave for 1 minute. Stir the mixture quickly until smooth ball of dough forms.

- Cut a piece of parchment for your work surface. Press the dough into a large rectangle on the parchment, wetting your hands to prevent the dough from sticking as necessary. Cut the dough into eight rectangles.

- On each rectangle place a few spoons of the meat mixture. Fold the short ends of each roll toward the center and roll the length as you would a burrito.

- Cut a piece of parchment to fit your air fryer basket. Place taco rolls onto the parchment and place into the air fryer basket.

- Adjust the temperature to 360°F (182°C) and air fry for 10 minutes.

- Flip halfway through the cooking time.

- Allow to cool 10 minutes before serving.

Per Serving

calories: 380 | fat: 26g | protein: 25g | carbs: 7g | net carbs: 5g | fiber: 2g

Prep time: 15 minutes | Cook time: 15 minutes | Makes 8 poppers

Ingredients:

- 8 medium jalapeño peppers, stemmed, halved, and seeded
- 1 (8-ounce / 227-g) package cream cheese (or Kite Hill brand cream cheese style spread for dairy-free), softened
- 2 pounds (907 g) ground beef (85% lean)
- 1 teaspoon fine sea salt
- ½ teaspoon ground black pepper
- 8 slices thin-cut bacon
- Fresh cilantro leaves, for garnish

Directions:

> Spray the air fryer basket with avocado oil. Preheat the air fryer to 400°F (204°C).

> Stuff each jalapeño half with a few tablespoons of cream cheese. Place the halves back together again to form 8 jalapeños.

> Season the ground beef with the salt and pepper and mix with your hands to incorporate.

> Flatten about ¼ pound (113 g) of ground beef in the palm of

your hand and place a stuffed jalapeño in the center. Fold the beef around the jalapeño, forming an egg shape.

➢ Wrap the beef-covered jalapeño with a slice of bacon and secure it with a toothpick.

➢ Place the jalapeños in the air fryer basket, leaving space between them (if you're using a smaller air fryer, work in batches if necessary), and air fry for 15 minutes, or until the beef is cooked through and the bacon is crispy.

➢ Garnish with cilantro before serving.

➢ Store leftovers in an airtight container in the fridge for 3 days or in the freezer for up to a month.

➢ Reheat in a preheated 350°F (177°C) air fryer for 4 minutes, or until heated through and the bacon is crispy.

Per Serving

calories: 679 | fat: 53g | protein: 42g | carbs: 3g | net carbs: 2g | fiber: 1g

Northern Meatloaf

Prep time: 10 minutes | Cook time: 35 minutes | Serves 8

Ingredients:

- 1½ pounds (680 g) ground beef (85% lean)
- ¼ pound (113 g) ground pork
- 1 large egg (organic or free range)
- ½ cup minced onions
- ¼ cup tomato sauce
- 2 tablespoons dry mustard
- 2 cloves garlic, minced
- 2 teaspoons fine sea salt
- 1 teaspoon ground black pepper, plus more for garnish

Sauce:

- ½ cup (1 stick) unsalted butter
- ½ cup shredded Swiss or mild Cheddar cheese (about 2 ounces / 57 g)
- 2 ounces (57 g) cream cheese (¼ cup), softened
- ⅓ cup beef broth
- ⅛ teaspoon ground nutmeg
- Halved cherry tomatoes, for serving (optional)

Directions:

➤ Preheat the air fryer to 390°F (199°C).

➤ In a large bowl, combine the ground beef, ground pork, egg, onions, tomato sauce, dry mustard, garlic, salt, and pepper. Using your hands, mix until well combined.

➤ Place the meatloaf mixture in a loaf pan and place it in the air fryer. Bake for 35 minutes, or until cooked through and the internal temperature reaches 145°F (63°C). Check the meatloaf after 25 minutes; if it's getting too brown on the top, cover it loosely with foil to prevent burning.

➤ While the meatloaf cooks, make the sauce: Heat the butter in a saucepan over medium-high heat until it sizzles and brown flecks appear, stirring constantly to keep the butter from burning.

➤ Turn the heat down to low and whisk in the Swiss cheese, cream cheese, broth, and nutmeg. Simmer for at least 10 minutes. The longer it simmers, the more the flavors open up. When the meatloaf is done, transfer it to a serving tray and pour the sauce over it.

➤ Garnish with ground black pepper and serve with cherry tomatoes, if desired. Allow the meatloaf to rest for 10 minutes before slicing so it doesn't crumble apart.

➤ Store leftovers in an airtight container in the fridge for 3 days or in the freezer for up to a month.

➤ Reheat in a preheated 350°F (177°C) air fryer for 4 minutes, or until heated through.

Per Serving

calories: 395 | fat: 32g | protein: 23g | carbs: 3g | net carbs: 2g | fiber: 1g

Salisbury Steak with Mushroom Onion Gravy

Prep time: 10 minutes | Cook time: 33 minutes | Serves 2

Ingredients:

Mushroom Onion Gravy:

- ¾ cup sliced button mushrooms
- ¼ cup thinly sliced onions
- ¼ cup unsalted butter, melted (or bacon fat for dairy-free)
- ½ teaspoon fine sea salt
- ¼ cup beef broth

Steaks:

- ½ pound (227 g) ground beef (85% lean)
- ¼ cup minced onions, or ½ teaspoon onion powder
- 2 tablespoons tomato paste
- 1 tablespoon dry mustard
- 1 clove garlic, minced, or ¼ teaspoon garlic powder
- ½ teaspoon fine sea salt
- ¼ teaspoon ground black pepper, plus more for garnish if desired Chopped fresh thyme leaves, for garnish (optional)

Directions:

➤ Preheat the air fryer to 390°F (199°C).

- ➤ Make the gravy: Place the mushrooms and onions in a casserole dish that will fit in your air fryer. Pour the melted butter over them and stir to coat, then season with the salt.

- ➤ Place the dish in the air fryer and bake for 5 minutes, stir, then cook for another 3 minutes, or until the onions are soft and the mushrooms are browning.

- ➤ Add the broth and cook for another 10 minutes.

- ➤ While the gravy is cooking, prepare the steaks: In a large bowl, mix together the ground beef, onions, tomato paste, dry mustard, garlic, salt, and pepper until well combined.

- ➤ Form the mixture into 2 oval-shaped patties. Place the patties on top of the mushroom gravy.

- ➤ Air fry for 10 minutes, gently flip the patties, then cook for another 2 to 5 minutes, until the beef is cooked through and the internal temperature reaches 145°F (63°C).

- ➤ Transfer the steaks to a serving platter and pour the gravy over them. Garnish with ground black pepper and chopped fresh thyme, if desired.

- ➤ Store leftovers in an airtight container in the fridge for 3 days or in the freezer for up to a month.

- ➤ Reheat in a preheated 350°F (177°C) air fryer for 4 minutes, or until heated through.

Per Serving

calories: 588 | fat: 44g | protein: 33g | carbs: 11g | net carbs: 8g | fiber: 3g

Tasty Fajita Meatball Lettuce Wraps

Prep time: 10 minutes | Cook time: 10 minutes | Serves 4

Ingredients:

- 1 pound (454 g) ground beef (85% lean)
- ½ cup salsa, plus more for serving if desired
- ¼ cup chopped onions
- ¼ cup diced green or red bell peppers
- 1 large egg (organic or free range), beaten
- 1 teaspoon fine sea salt
- ½ teaspoon chili powder
- ½ teaspoon ground cumin
- 1 clove garlic, minced For Serving (Optional):
- 8 leaves Boston lettuce Pico de gallo or salsa Lime slices

Directions:

- ➢ Spray the air fryer basket with avocado oil. Preheat the air fryer to 350°F (177°C).

- ➢ In a large bowl, mix together all the ingredients until well combined.

- ➢ Shape the meat mixture into eight 1-inch balls.

- ➢ Place the meatballs in the air fryer basket, leaving a little space between them.

- ➢ Air fry for 10 minutes, or until cooked through and no longer pink inside and the internal temperature reaches 145°F (63°C).

- ➢ Serve each meatball on a lettuce leaf, topped with pico de gallo or salsa, if desired.

- ➢ Serve with lime slices if desired.

- ➢ Store leftovers in an airtight container in the fridge for 3 days or in the freezer for up to a month.

- ➢ Reheat in a preheated 350°F (177°C) air fryer for 4 minutes, or until heated through.

Per Serving

calories: 272 | fat: 18g | protein: 23g | carbs: 3g | net carbs: 2g | fiber: 1g

Prep time: 10 minutes | Cook time: 10 minutes | Serves 4

Ingredients:

- 1½ pounds (680 g) venison or beef tenderloin, pounded
- to ¼ inch thick
- 3 teaspoons fine sea salt
- 1 teaspoon ground black pepper
- 2 ounces (57 g) creamy goat cheese
- ½ cup crumbled feta cheese (about 2 ounces / 57 g)
- ¼ cup finely chopped onions
- 2 cloves garlic, minced
- For Garnish/Serving (Optional):
- Prepared yellow mustard Halved cherry tomatoes Extra-virgin olive oil Sprigs of fresh rosemary Lavender flowers

Directions:

➢ Spray the air fryer basket with avocado oil. Preheat the air fryer to 400°F (204°C).

➢ Season the tenderloin on all sides with the salt and pepper.

➢ In a medium-sized mixing bowl, combine the goat cheese, feta, onions, and garlic.

➢ Place the mixture in the center of the tenderloin. Starting at the end closest to you, tightly roll the tenderloin like a jelly roll.

➢ Tie the rolled tenderloin tightly with kitchen twine.

➢ Place the meat in the air fryer basket and air fry for 5 minutes. Flip the meat over and cook for another 5 minutes, or until the internal temperature reaches 135°F (57°C) for medium-rare.

➢ To serve, smear a line of prepared yellow mustard on a platter, then place the meat next to it and add halved cherry tomatoes on the side, if desired.

➢ Drizzle with olive oil and garnish with rosemary sprigs and lavender flowers, if desired.

➢ Best served fresh. Store leftovers in an airtight container in the fridge for 3 days. Reheat in a preheated 350°F (177°C) air fryer for 4 minutes, or until heated through.

Per Serving

calories: 415 | fat: 16g | protein: 62g | carbs: 4g | net carbs: 3g | fiber: 1g

Herb-Crusted and Parmesan Lamb Chops

Prep time: 10 minutes | Cook time: 5 minutes | Serves 2

Ingredients:

- 1 large egg (organic or free range)
- 2 cloves garlic, minced
- ¼ cup pork dust
- ¼ cup powdered Parmesan cheese
- 1 tablespoon chopped fresh oregano leaves
- 1 tablespoon chopped fresh rosemary leaves
- 1 teaspoon chopped fresh thyme leaves
- ½ teaspoon ground black pepper
- 4 (1-inch-thick) lamb chops
- For Garnish/Serving (Optional):
- Sprigs of fresh oregano Sprigs of fresh rosemary Sprigs of fresh thyme Lavender flowers Lemon slices

Directions:

➢ Spray the air fryer basket with avocado oil. Preheat the air fryer to 400°F (204°C).

➢ Beat the egg in a shallow bowl, add the garlic, and stir well to combine. In another shallow bowl, mix together the pork dust, Parmesan, herbs, and pepper.

➢ One at a time, dip the lamb chops into the egg mixture,

shake off the excess egg, and then dredge them in the Parmesan mixture.

➤ Use your hands to coat the chops well in the Parmesan mixture and form a nice crust on all sides; if necessary, dip the chops again in both the egg and the

Parmesan mixture.

➤ Place the lamb chops in the air fryer basket, leaving space between them, and air fry for 5 minutes, or until the internal temperature reaches 145°F (63°C) for medium doneness. Allow to rest for 10 minutes before serving.

➤ Garnish with sprigs of oregano, rosemary, and thyme, and lavender flowers, if desired. Serve with lemon slices, if desired.

➤ Best served fresh. Store leftovers in an airtight container in the fridge for up to 4 days.

➤ Serve chilled over a salad, or reheat in a 350°F (177°C) air fryer for 3 minutes, or until heated through.

Per Serving

calories: 790 | fat: 60g | protein: 57g | carbs: 2g | net carbs: 1g | fiber: 1g

Air Fryer Mojito Lamb Chops

Prep time: 5 minutes | Cook time: 5 minutes | Serves 2

Ingredients:

Marinade:

- 2 teaspoons grated lime zest
- ½ cup lime juice
- ¼ cup avocado oil
- ¼ cup chopped fresh mint leaves
- 4 cloves garlic, roughly chopped
- 2 teaspoons fine sea salt
- ½ teaspoon ground black pepper
- 4 (1-inch-thick) lamb chops
- Sprigs of fresh mint, for garnish (optional)
- Lime slices, for serving (optional)

Directions:

➢ Make the marinade: Place all the ingredients for the marinade in a food processor or blender and purée until mostly smooth with a few small chunks.

➢ Transfer half of the marinade to a shallow dish and set the other half aside for serving. Add the lamb to the shallow dish, cover, and place in the refrigerator to marinate for at least 2 hours or overnight.

➢ Spray the air fryer basket with avocado oil. Preheat the air fryer to 390°F (199°C).

➤ Remove the chops from the marinade and place them in the air fryer basket.

➤ Air fry for 5 minutes, or until the internal temperature reaches 145°F (63°C) for medium doneness.

➤ Allow the chops to rest for 10 minutes before serving with the rest of the marinade as a sauce.

➤ Garnish with fresh mint leaves and serve with lime slices, if desired. Best served fresh.

Per Serving

calories: 692 | fat: 53g | protein: 48g | carbs: 5g | net carbs: 4g | fiber: 1g

Prep time: 10 minutes | Cook time: 7 minutes | Serves 4

Ingredients:

- 4 hot dogs
- 2 large dill pickles
- ¼ cup diced onions
- tomato, cut into ½-inch dice
- 4 pickled peppers, diced For Garnish
- (Optional): Brown mustard Celery salt Poppy seeds

Directions:

- ➤ Spray the air fryer basket with avocado oil. Preheat the air fryer to 400°F (204°C).

- ➤ Place the hot dogs in the air fryer basket and air fry for 5 to 7 minutes, until hot and slightly crispy.

- ➤ While the hot dogs cook, quarter one of the dill pickles lengthwise, so that you have 4 pickle spears.

- ➤ Finely dice the other pickle.

- ➤ When the hot dogs are done, transfer them to a serving platter and arrange them in a row, alternating with the pickle spears. Top with the diced pickles, onions, tomato, and sport peppers.

- ➤ Drizzle brown mustard on top and garnish with celery salt and poppy seeds, if desired.

- ➤ Best served fresh. Store leftover hot dogs in an airtight container in the refrigerator for up to 3 days.

- ➤ Reheat in a preheated 390°F (199°C) air fryer for 2 minutes, or until warmed through.

Per Serving

calories: 123 | fat: 8g | protein: 8g | carbs: 3g | net carbs: 2g | fiber: 1g

Air Fryer Pork Milanese

Prep time: 10 minutes | Cook time: 12 minutes | Serves 4

Ingredients:

- 4 (1-inch) boneless pork chops
- Fine sea salt and ground black pepper, to taste
- 2 large eggs (organic or free range)
- ¾ cup powdered Parmesan cheese
- Chopped fresh parsley, for garnish
- Lemon slices, for serving

Directions:

- ➢ Spray the air fryer basket with avocado oil. Preheat the air fryer to 400°F (204°C).

- ➢ Place the pork chops between 2 sheets of plastic wrap and pound them with the flat side of a meat tenderizer until they're ¼ inch thick.

- ➢ Lightly season both sides of the chops with salt and pepper.

- ➢ Lightly beat the eggs in a shallow bowl. Divide the Parmesan cheese evenly between 2 bowls and set the bowls in this order: Parmesan, eggs, Parmesan.

- ➢ Dredge a chop in the first bowl of Parmesan, then dip it in the eggs, and then dredge it again in the second bowl of

Parmesan, making sure both sides and all edges are well coated.

➢ Repeat with the remaining chops.

➢ Place the chops in the air fryer basket and air fry for 12 minutes, or until the internal temperature reaches 145°F (63°C), flipping halfway through.

➢ Garnish with fresh parsley and serve immediately with lemon slices.

➢ Store leftovers in an airtight container in the refrigerator for up to 3 days.

➢ Reheat in a preheated 390°F (199°C) air fryer for 5 minutes, or until warmed through.

Per Serving

calories: 351 | fat: 18g | protein: 42g | carbs: 3g | net carbs: 2g | fiber: 1g

Italian Sausages with Peppers, Onions and Mustard

Prep time: 5 minutes | Cook time: 28 minutes | Serves 3

Ingredients:

- 1 medium onion, thinly sliced
- 1 yellow or orange bell pepper, thinly sliced
- 1 red bell pepper, thinly sliced
- ¼ cup avocado oil or melted coconut oil
- 1 teaspoon fine sea salt
- 6 Italian sausages
- Dijon mustard, for serving (optional)

Directions:

➤ Preheat the air fryer to 400°F (204°C).

➤ Place the onion and peppers in a large bowl. Drizzle with the oil and toss well to coat the veggies. Season with the salt.

➤ Place the onion and peppers in a pie pan and cook in the air fryer for 8 minutes, stirring halfway through.

➤ Remove from the air fryer and set aside.

➤ Spray the air fryer basket with avocado oil. Place the sausages in the air fryer basket and air fry for 20 minutes, or until crispy and golden brown.

➤ During the last minute or two of cooking, add the onion and peppers to the basket with the sausages to warm them through.

➤ Place the onion and peppers on a serving platter and arrange the sausages on top.

➤ Serve Dijon mustard on the side, if desired.

➤ Store leftovers in an airtight container in the fridge for up to 7 days or in the freezer for up to a month.

➤ Reheat in a preheated 390°F (199°C) air fryer for 3 minutes, or until heated through.

Per Serving

calories: 576 | fat: 49g | protein: 25g | carbs: 8g | net carbs: 6g | fiber: 2g

Pork Tenderloin with Avocado Lime Sauce and Paprika

Prep time: 10 minutes | Cook time: 15 minutes | Serves 4

Ingredients:

Marinade:

- ½ cup lime juice Grated zest of 1 lime
- 2 teaspoons stevia glycerite, or ¼ teaspoon liquid stevia
- 3 cloves garlic, minced
- 1½ teaspoons fine sea salt
- 1 teaspoon chili powder, or more for more heat
- 1 teaspoon smoked paprika
- 1 pound (454 g) pork tenderloin

Avocado Lime Sauce:

- 1 medium-sized ripe avocado, roughly chopped
- ½ cup full-fat sour cream (or coconut cream for dairy-free) Grated zest of 1 lime
- Juice of 1 lime
- 2 cloves garlic, roughly chopped
- ½ teaspoon fine sea salt
- ¼ teaspoon ground black pepper Chopped fresh cilantro leaves,
- for garnish Lime slices, for serving
- Pico de gallo, for serving

Directions:

➢ In a medium-sized casserole dish, stir together all the marinade ingredients until well combined. Add the tenderloin and coat it well in the marinade. Cover and place in the fridge to marinate for 2 hours or overnight.

➢ Spray the air fryer basket with avocado oil. Preheat the air fryer to 400°F (204°C).

➢ Remove the pork from the marinade and place it in the air fryer basket. Air fry for 13 to 15 minutes, until the internal temperature of the pork is 145°F (63°C), flipping after 7 minutes.

➢ Remove the pork from the air fryer and place it on a cutting board. Allow it to rest for 8 to 10 minutes, then cut it into ½-inch-thick slices.

➢ While the pork cooks, make the avocado lime sauce: Place all the sauce ingredients in a food processor and purée until smooth. Taste and adjust the seasoning to your liking.

➢ Place the pork slices on a serving platter and spoon the avocado lime sauce on top. Garnish with cilantro leaves and serve with lime slices and pico de gallo.

➢ Store leftovers in an airtight container in the fridge for up to 4 days. Reheat in a preheated 400°F (204°C) air fryer for 5 minutes, or until heated through.

Per Serving

calories: 326 | fat: 19g | protein: 26g | carbs: 15g | net carbs: 9g | fiber: 6g

Delicious Marinated Steak Tips with Mushrooms

Prep time: 10 minutes | Cook time: 10 minutes | Serves 4

Ingredients:

- 1½ pounds (680 g) sirloin, trimmed and cut into 1-inch pieces

- 8 ounces (227 g) brown mushrooms, halved

- ¼ cup Worcestershire sauce

- 1 tablespoon Dijon mustard

- 1 tablespoon olive oil

- 1 teaspoon paprika

- 1 teaspoon crushed red pepper flakes

- 2 tablespoons chopped fresh parsley (optional)

Directions:

➢ Place the beef and mushrooms in a gallon-size resealable bag. I

➢ n a small bowl, whisk together the Worcestershire, mustard, olive oil, paprika, and red pepper flakes.

➢ Pour the marinade into the bag and massage gently to ensure the beef and mushrooms are evenly coated.

➢ Seal the bag and refrigerate for at least 4 hours, preferably overnight.

➢ Remove from the refrigerator 30 minutes before cooking.

➢ Preheat the air fryer to 400°F (204°C).

➢ Drain and discard the marinade.

➢ Arrange the steak and mushrooms in the air fryer basket.

➢ Air fry for 10 minutes, pausing halfway through the baking time to shake the basket.

➢ Transfer to a serving plate and top with the parsley, if desired.

Per Serving

calories: 330 | fat: 17g | protein: 41g | carbs: 2g | net carbs: 2g | fiber: 0g

Prep time: 5 minutes | Cook time: 20 to 25 minutes | Serves 4

Ingredients:

- 4 thick center-cut boneless pork chops (about 1½ pounds / 680 g)
- 1 tablespoon olive oil
- 1 teaspoon salt
- 1 (15-ounce / 425-g) can crushed tomatoes
- 1 tablespoon Italian seasoning
- 2 cloves garlic, minced
- ¼ cup chopped kalamata olives
- 2 tablespoons chopped fresh parsley

Directions:

- ➤ Preheat the air fryer to 400°F (204°C).

- ➤ Arrange the pork chops in a round baking dish.

- ➤ Drizzle with the olive oil and season both sides with the salt.

- ➤ In a bowl, combine the tomatoes, Italian seasoning, and garlic. Pour the tomato mixture over the pork chops.

- ➤ Pausing halfway through the cooking time to turn the chops, air fry for 20 to 25 minutes, until a thermometer inserted into the thickest piece registers 145°F (63°C).

➢ Remove the chops from the sauce and let rest for 5 minutes. Stir the olives and parsley into the sauce before serving with the pork chops.

Per Serving

calories: 350 | fat: 17g | protein: 40g | carbs: 9g | net carbs: 7g | fiber: 2g

Prep time: 5 minutes | Cook time: 30 to 35 minutes | Serves 8

Ingredients:

- 1 (2-pound / 907-g) top round beef roast, tied with kitchen string
- Sea salt and freshly ground black pepper, to taste
- 2 teaspoons minced garlic
- 2 tablespoons finely chopped fresh rosemary
- ¼ cup avocado oil

Directions:

- ➢ Season the roast generously with salt and pepper.

- ➢ In a small bowl, whisk together the garlic, rosemary, and avocado oil. Rub this all over the roast.

- ➢ Cover loosely with aluminum foil or plastic wrap and refrigerate for at least 12 hours or up to 2 days.

- ➢ Remove the roast from the refrigerator and allow to sit at room temperature for about 1 hour.

- ➢ Set the air fryer to 325°F (163°C). Place the roast in the air fryer basket and roast for 15 minutes.

- ➢ Flip the roast and cook for 15 to 20 minutes more, until the meat is browned and an instant-read thermometer reads 120°F (49°C) at the thickest part (for medium-rare).

- ➢ Transfer the meat to a cutting board, and let it rest for 15 minutes before thinly slicing and serving.

Per Serving

calories: 213 | fat: 10g | protein: 25g | carbs: 2g | net carbs: 1g | fiber: 1g

Tenderloin with Crispy Shallots

Prep time: 5 minutes | Cook time: 18 to 20 minutes | Serves 6

Ingredients:

- 1½ pounds (680 g) beef tenderloin steaks
- Sea salt and freshly ground black pepper, to taste
- 4 medium shallots
- teaspoon olive oil or avocado oil

Directions:

➢ Season both sides of the steaks with salt and pepper, and let them sit at room temperature for 45 minutes.

➢ Set the air fryer to 400°F (204°C) and let it preheat for 5 minutes.

➢ Working in batches if necessary, place the steaks in the air fryer basket in a single layer and air fry for 5 minutes.

➢ Flip and cook for 5 minutes longer, until an instant-read thermometer inserted in the center of the steaks registers 120°F (49°C) for medium-rare (or as desired).

➢ Remove the steaks and tent with aluminum foil to rest.

➢ Set the air fryer to 300°F (149°C). In a medium bowl, toss the shallots with the oil.

➢ Place the shallots in the basket and air fry for 5 minutes, then give them a toss and cook for 3 to 5 minutes more, until crispy and golden brown.

➤ Place the steaks on serving plates and arrange the shallots on top.

Per Serving

calories: 186 | fat: 5g | protein: 30g | carbs: 5g | net carbs: 5g | fiber: 0g

Sesame and Cumin Beef Lettuce Tacos

Prep time: 15 minutes | Cook time: 8 to 10 minutes | Serves 4

Ingredients:

- ¼ cup coconut aminos
- ¼ cup avocado oil
- 2 tablespoons cooking sherry
- 1 tablespoon Swerve
- 1 tablespoon ground cumin
- 1 teaspoon minced garlic
- Sea salt and freshly ground black pepper, to taste
- 1 pound (454 g) flank steak
- 8 butter lettuce leaves
- 2 scallions, sliced
- 1 tablespoon toasted sesame seeds
- Hot sauce, for serving
- Lime wedges, for serving
- Flaky sea salt (optional)

Directions:

> In a small bowl, whisk together the coconut aminos, avocado oil, cooking sherry, Swerve, cumin, garlic, and salt and pepper to taste.

> Place the steak in a shallow dish. Pour the marinade over the

beef. Cover the dish with plastic wrap and let it marinate in the refrigerator for at least 2 hours or overnight.

➢ Remove the flank steak from the dish and discard the marinade.

➢ Set the air fryer to 400°F (204°C). Place the steak in the air fryer basket and air fry for 4 to 6 minutes.

➢ Flip the steak and cook for 4 minutes more, until an instant-read thermometer reads 120°F (49°C) at the thickest part (or cook it to your desired doneness).

➢ Allow the steak to rest for 10 minutes, then slice it thinly against the grain.

➢ Stack 2 lettuce leaves on top of each other and add some sliced meat.

➢ Top with scallions and sesame seeds. Drizzle with hot sauce and lime juice, and finish with a little flaky salt (if using). Repeat with the remaining lettuce leaves and fillings.

Per Serving

calories: 349 | fat: 22g | protein: 25g | carbs: 10g | net carbs: 5g | fiber: 5g

Prep time: 25 minutes | Cook time: 36 minutes | Serves 6

Ingredients:

- 1 recipe Fathead Pizza Dough

- 1 pound (454 g) ground beef

- 2 tablespoons Taco Seasoning

- 1 canned chipotle chile in adobo sauce, diced and sauce removed

- ⅓ cup plus 1 tablespoon sugar-free salsa, divided

- 6 ounces (170 g) Cheddar cheese, grated

- 3 scallions, chopped

- ¼ cup sour cream

Directions:

➢ Divide the dough into three equal pieces. Place each piece between two sheets of parchment paper, and roll it into a 7-inch round.

➢ Place one dough round in a cake pan or air fryer pizza pan (or a similar pan that fits inside your air fryer). Place the pan in the air fryer basket.

➢ Set your air fryer to 375°F (191°C). Bake the dough for 6 minutes. Remove from the air fryer and repeat with the remaining dough.

> While the crusts are cooking, heat a large skillet over medium-high heat.

> Add the ground beef and cook, breaking the meat up with a spoon, for 5 minutes. Stir in the taco seasoning and chipotle chile, and cook until the meat is browned. Remove the skillet from the heat and stir in ⅓ cup of salsa.

> Divide the meat among the pizza crusts. Top with the cheese and scallions. Return one pizza to the air fryer and bake for 6 minutes, until the cheese is melted.

> Repeat with the remaining pizzas.

> Combine the sour cream and remaining 1 tablespoon of salsa in a small bowl. Drizzle this over the finished pizzas.

> If desired, top the pizzas with additional desired toppings, such as shredded romaine lettuce, pickled jalapeño slices, diced tomatoes, cilantro, and lime juice. Serve warm.

Per Serving

calories: 614 | fat: 52g | protein: 34g | carbs: 10g | net carbs: 6g | fiber: 4g

Notes for My Recipes and Change

Recipe Name

Recipe Name

Recipes Name

Notes for My Recipes and Changes

Recipe Name

Recipe Name

Recipes Name

Notes for My Recipes and Changes

Recipe Name

Recipe Name

Recipes Name

Notes for My Recipes and Changes

Recipe Name

Recipe Name

Recipes Name

Notes for My Recipes and Changes

Recipe Name

Recipe Name

Recipes Name

Notes for My Recipes and Changes

Recipe Name

Recipe Name

Recipes Name

Appendix 1: Measurement Conversion Chart

Beef

Item	Temp (°F)	Time (mins)	Item	Temp (°F)	Time (mins)
Beef Eye Round Roast (4 lbs.)	400 °F	45 to 55	Meatballs (1-inch)	370 °F	7
Burger Patty (4 oz.)	370 °F	16 to 20	Meatballs (3-inch)	380 °F	10
Filet Mignon (8 oz.)	400 °F	18	Ribeye, bone-in (1-inch, 8 oz)	400 °F	10 to 15
Flank Steak (1.5 lbs.)	400 °F	12	Sirloin steaks (1-inch, 12 oz)	400 °F	9 to 14
Flank Steak (2 lbs.)	400 °F	20 to 28			

Chicken

Item	Temp (°F)	Time (mins)	Item	Temp (°F)	Time (mins)
Breasts, bone in (1 ¼ lb.)	370 °F	25	Legs, bone-in (1 ¾ lb.)	380 °F	30
Breasts, boneless (4 oz)	380 °F	12	Thighs, boneless (1 ½ lb.)	380 °F	18 to 20
Drumsticks (2 ½ lb.)	370 °F	20	Wings (2 lb.)	400 °F	12
Game Hen (halved 2 lb.)	390 °F	20	Whole Chicken	360 °F	75
Thighs, bone-in (2 lb.)	380 °F	22	Tenders	360 °F	8 to 10

Pork & Lamb

Item	Temp (°F)	Time (mins)	Item	Temp (°F)	Time (mins)
Bacon (regular)	400 °F	5 to 7	Pork Tenderloin	370 °F	15
Bacon (thick cut)	400 °F	6 to 10	Sausages	380 °F	15
Pork Loin (2 lb.)	360 °F	55	Lamb Loin Chops (1-inch thick)	400 °F	8 to 12
Pork Chops, bone in (1-inch, 6.5 oz)	400 °F	12	Rack of Lamb (1.5 – 2 lb.)	380 °F	22

Fish & Seafood

Item	Temp (°F)	Time (mins)	Item	Temp (°F)	Time (mins)
Calamari (8 oz)	400 °F	4	Tuna Steak	400 °F	7 to 10
Fish Fillet (1-inch, 8 oz)	400 °F	10	Scallops	400 °F	5 to 7
Salmon, fillet (6 oz)	380 °F	12	Shrimp	400 °F	5
Swordfish steak	400 °F	10			

Appendix 2: Air Fryer Cooking Chart

VOLUME EQUIVALENTS(DRY)

US STANDARD	METRIC (APPROXIMATE)
1/8 teaspoon	0.5 mL
1/4 teaspoon	1 mL
1/2 teaspoon	2 mL
3/4 teaspoon	4 mL
1 teaspoon	5 mL
1 tablespoon	15 mL
1/4 cup	59 mL
1/2 cup	118 mL
3/4 cup	177 mL
1 cup	235 mL
2 cups	475 mL
3 cups	700 mL
4 cups	1 L

VOLUME EQUIVALENTS(LIQUID)

US STANDARD	US STANDARD (OUNCES)	METRIC (APPROXIMATE)
2 tablespoons	1 fl.oz.	30 mL
1/4 cup	2 fl.oz.	60 mL
1/2 cup	4 fl.oz.	120 mL
1 cup	8 fl.oz.	240 mL
1 1/2 cup	12 fl.oz.	355 mL
2 cups or 1 pint	16 fl.oz.	475 mL
4 cups or 1 quart	32 fl.oz.	1 L
1 gallon	128 fl.oz.	4 L

TEMPERATURES EQUIVALENTS

FAHRENHEIT(F)	CELSIUS(C) (APPROXIMATE)
225 °F	107 °C
250 °F	120 °C
275 °F	135 °C
300 °F	150 °C
325 °F	160 °C
350 °F	180 °C
375 °F	190 °C
400 °F	205 °C
425 °F	220 °C
450 °F	235 °C
475 °F	245 °C
500 °F	260 °C

WEIGHT EQUIVALENTS

US STANDARD	METRIC (APPROXIMATE)
1 ounce	28 g
2 ounces	57 g
5 ounces	142 g
10 ounces	284 g
15 ounces	425 g
16 ounces (1 pound)	455 g
1.5 pounds	680 g
2 pounds	907 g

Vegetables

INGREDIENT	AMOUNT	PREPARATION	OIL	TEMP	COOK TIME
Asparagus	2 bunches	Cut in half, trim stems	2 Tbsp	420°F	12-15 mins
Beets	1½ lbs	Peel, cut in ½-inch cubes	1Tbsp	390°F	28-30 mins
Bell peppers (for roasting)	4 peppers	Cut in quarters, remove seeds	1Tbsp	400°F	15-20 mins
Broccoli	1 large head	Cut in 1-2-inch florets	1Tbsp	400°F	15-20 mins
Brussels sprouts	1lb	Cut in half, remove stems	1Tbsp	425°F	15-20 mins
Carrots	1lb	Peel, cut in ¼-inch rounds	1 Tbsp	425°F	10-15 mins
Cauliflower	1 head	Cut in 1-2-inch florets	2 Tbsp	400°F	20-22 mins
Corn on the cob	7 ears	Whole ears, remove husks	1 Tbps	400°F	14-17 mins
Green beans	1 bag (12 oz)	Trim	1 Tbps	420°F	18-20 mins
Kale (for chips)	4 oz	Tear into pieces,remove stems	None	325°F	5-8 mins
Mushrooms	16 oz	Rinse, slice thinly	1 Tbps	390°F	25-30 mins
Potatoes, russet	1½ lbs	Cut in 1-inch wedges	1 Tbps	390°F	25-30 mins
Potatoes, russet	1lb	Hand-cut fries, soak 30 mins in cold water, then pat dry	½ -3 Tbps	400°F	25-28 mins
Potatoes, sweet	1lb	Hand-cut fries, soak 30 mins in cold water, then pat dry	1 Tbps	400°F	25-28 mins
Zucchini	1lb	Cut in eighths lengthwise, then cut in half	1 Tbps	400°F	15-20 mins

CPSIA information can be obtained
at www.ICGtesting.com
Printed in the USA
BVHW022106260721
612929BV00020B/1038

9 781914 061622

MARTIN XB-48 MEDIUM BOMBER

BACKGROUND: In April 1944, the United States Army Air Forces (USAAF) issued requirements for a jet-propelled medium bomber. The specifications were somewhat general and called for an 80,000 to 200,000 lbs gross weight, a 40,000 ft ceiling, a 1,000 mile combat radius, possess a maximum speed of 500 mph and be powered by TG-180 (J35) or TG-190 (J47) jet engines. On 17 November 1944, these specifications were amended to: ceiling of 45,000 ft, range of 3,000 miles, and maximum speed of 550 mph.

The Glenn L. Martin company submitted its Model 223 in response

to these specifications to the Air Technical Service Command on 9 December 1944. Martin's proposal was accepted on 29 December 1944 and Letter Contract W33-038 ac-7675 was issued to Martin for one mock-up of what was to become the XB-48. The letter contract of December for $574,826 was superceded by a definitive contract on 27 March 1945 with a revised cost of $569,252.

Four manufacturers submitted designs, all of which were awarded contracts. The four were: North American XB-45 (see Air Force Legends #224); Consolidated Vultee,

Above and below, artist's rendition of the final XB-48 design. (GLMMAM Archive)

XB-46 (see Air Force Legends #221); Boeing XB-47; and the Martin XB-48. On 29 January 1945, an armament stipulation was issued to all manufacturers which called-out specific bomb loads, including the M-121 "Dam-Buster" 10,000 lb bomb and the 22,000 lb "Grand Slam" bomb. In March 1946, Martin offered to produce one stripped and one complete XB-48 for a fixed-price of $10 million. After further negotiations, a final con-

Above, Boeing XB-47, S/N 46-065, during its roll-out at Seattle in September 1947. (Norman Taylor collection) Below, Consolidated Vultee XB-46, S/N 45-59582, over Muroc Dry Lake bed on 26 May 1947. (Craig Kaston collection) Bottom, North American RB-45C, S/N 48-024, over Southern California in July 1950. (USAF)

tract (W33-038 ac-13492) was approved on 13 December 1946. The new contract was for $10.9 million and called for two XB-48s, spare parts, and a bomb bay mock up. The contract also called for wind tunnel tests to be completed

by 1 January 1947, delivery of ship one by 30 September 1947, and delivery of ship two by 30 June 1948.

Boeing was allowed to apply German swept-wing data to its entry which promised much greater performance over the other three straight wing designs. From the start, North American's XB-45 was favored over the XB-46 and XB-48 relegating them to backup designs. In the end, North American received an initial contract for 96 B-45A aircraft and Boeing's XB-47 was allowed continued funding which ultimately produced the world's best medium bomber of the 1950s.

All four manufacturers' aircraft initially flew with TG-180 (J35) engines. The XB-45/B-45A and the XB-46 utilized four engines in two underwing pods and the XB-47 and XB-48 were fitted with six of these engines. Starting with the B-45A-5s, TG-190 (J47) engines replaced the TG-180 (J35) units. Only the first XB-47 prototype flew with TG-180 (J35)s. All subsequent XB-47/B-47s were fitted with TG-190 (J47)s. The Boeing design had two twin and two single underwing engine pods and the Martin XB-48 utilized two three-engine under wing pod clusters for its six TG-180 (J35)s.

GENERAL DESCRIPTION: The Martin Model 233, XB-48, was a three-place, six-turbojet engine, high-wing, all metal medium bomber. The landing gear consisted of dual wheel main gear located in tandem with outrigger single wheel type wing gear. The main gear, wing gear, nose gear steering, and wing flaps were hydraulically operated by a 3,000 psi system. The bomb bay doors and brakes were pneumatically operated. All control surfaces were hydraulically boosted. These included the ailerons, which consisted of small "feel" ailerons and "spoiler" ailerons; the rudder; and the elevators. A 22,000 lb capacity horizontal bomb bay with quick-acting doors which retracted within the fuselage contours. Defensive armament consisted of a remote controlled tail turret with two .50 caliber machine guns. Proposed radar was for a 60" scanner.

MARTIN XB-48 MEDIUM BOMBER SPECIFICATIONS

Length	85'9"	Ailerons Down Travel, Feel	20°
Span	108'5"		
Height	27'5"	WING FLAPS:	
Height to top of canopy	10'1"	Inboard Flaps (down)	55°
Fuselage Width	9'1"	Outboard Flaps (down)	55°
Weight Empty (lbs)	63,603		
Weight Combat (lbs)	77,645		
Weight Maximum Take-Off (lbs)	102,600	ELEVATORS:	
		Elevators Up	25°
WING:		Elevator Down	15°
Airfoil Section (NACA 65 Series Modified)	GLM W-17		
Airfoil Thickness	11%	RUDDER:	
Wing Area (sq. ft.)	1,330	Right Rudder	20°
Wing Loading (lbs per sq. ft.)	77.1	Left Rudder	20°
Root Chord (inches)	220.0		
Tip Chord (inches)	91.0	TRIM TABS:	
Taper Ratio	2.42	Trim Aileron Up (Flap)	15°
Incidence at Root	3.3°	Trim Aileron Down (Flap)	15°
Incidence at Tip	3.5°		
Dihedral (Chord Plane)	0.0°	TAB, FEEL AILERON:	
Sweepback (Leading Edge Chord)	2°24'2"	Left Side Up	10°
Maximum Rib Spacing (inches)	173.0	Left Side Down	10°
Aspect Ratio	8.82	Right Side	No Trim Function
M.A.C. (inches)	157.0		
		TAB, ELEVATOR:	
HORIZONTAL TAIL:		Up	10°
Area at Chord Plane (sq. ft.)	362.3	Down	20°
Span at Chord Plane (sq. ft.)	42.2		
Maximum Chord (inches)	138.0	TAB, RUDDER:	
Airfoil (NACA)	65-011	Right (tolerance of +3°, -0°)	20°
		Left (tolerance of +3°, -0°)	20°
STABILIZER:			
Area Forward of Hinge Line (sq. ft.)	249.7	PERFORMANCE: Condition, 500 lb Bombs	
Incidense Relative to Longitudinel Axis	+ 45°	High Speed at 35,000 ft.	531 mph
Dihedral	10°	Maximum Range (miles)	3,525
		Average Cruising Speed for Above Range	464 mph
ELEVATOR:		Service Ceiling	41,500 ft.
Area Aft of Hinge Line (sq. ft.)	112.6	Take-Off Distance (over 50 ft. obstacle)	5,925 ft.
Area of Horn Balances (sq. ft.)	12.0	Landing Distance (over 50 ft. obstacle)	3,500 ft.
VERTICAL TAIL SURFACES:		PERFORMANCE: Condition, 22,000 lb Bomb	
Area (sq. ft.)	132.5	High Speed at 35,000 ft.	528 mph
Span (inches)	183.0	Maximum Range (miles)	2,790
Maximum Chord (inches)	140.0	Average Cruising Speed for Above Range	464 mph
Airfoil (NACA)	65-011	Service Ceiling	40,000 ft.
Area Dorsal Fin (sq. ft.)	13.0	Take-Off Distance (over 50 ft. obstacle)	5,925 ft.
		Landing Distance (over 50 ft. obstacle)	3,500 ft.
RUDDER:			
Area Aft of Hinge Line (sq. ft.)	34.4	PERFORMANCE: Condition, Ferry with 10,290 gals Fuel	
		High Speed at 35,000 ft.	532 mph
CONTROL SURFACES RANGE of MOVEMENT		Maximum Range (miles)	3,890
Stabilizor Setting (minutes)	+ 45	Average Cruising Speed for Above Range	466 mph
Fin, Normal Setting	0°	Service Ceiling	42,000 ft.
		Take-Off Distance (over 50 ft. obstacle)	5,925 ft.
		Landing Distance (over 50 ft. obstacle)	3,500 ft.
AILERONS:			
Ailerons Up Travel, Basic	35°		
Ailerons Down Travel, Basic	0°	Rate-of-Climb at 86,000 lbs	4,200 fpm
Ailerons Up Travel, Feel	20°	Rate-of-Climb at 102,000 lbs	3,250 fpm

XB-48 ACCESS PANELS

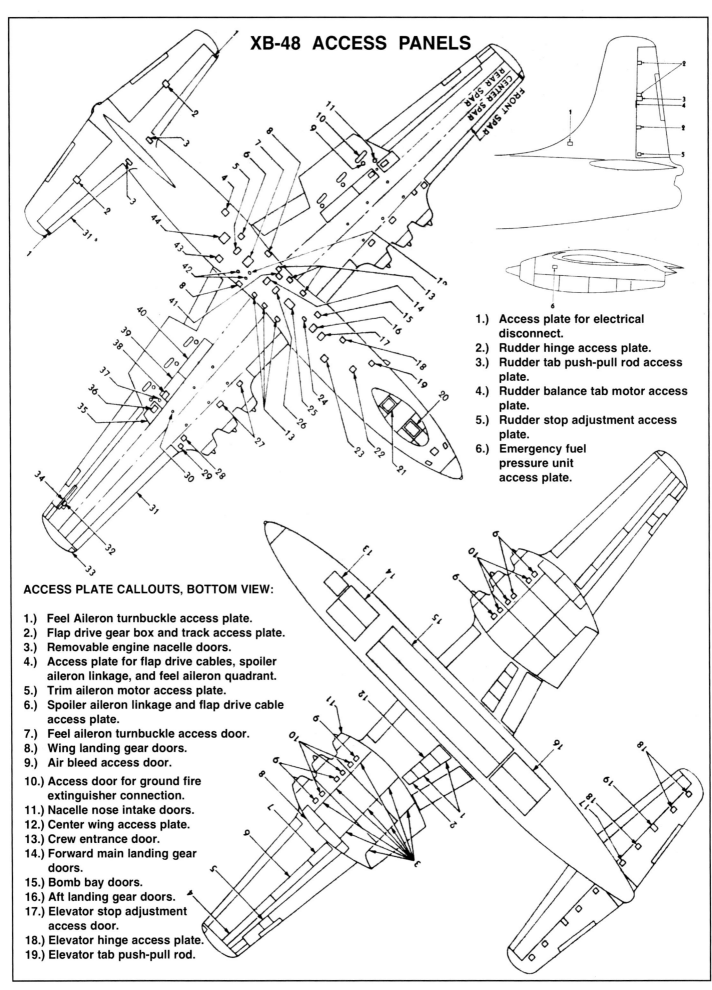

1.) Access plate for electrical disconnect.
2.) Rudder hinge access plate.
3.) Rudder tab push-pull rod access plate.
4.) Rudder balance tab motor access plate.
5.) Rudder stop adjustment access plate.
6.) Emergency fuel pressure unit access plate.

ACCESS PLATE CALLOUTS, BOTTOM VIEW:

1.) Feel Aileron turnbuckle access plate.
2.) Flap drive gear box and track access plate.
3.) Removable engine nacelle doors.
4.) Access plate for flap drive cables, spoiler aileron linkage, and feel aileron quadrant.
5.) Trim aileron motor access plate.
6.) Spoiler aileron linkage and flap drive cable access plate.
7.) Feel aileron turnbuckle access door.
8.) Wing landing gear doors.
9.) Air bleed access door.
10.) Access door for ground fire extinguisher connection.
11.) Nacelle nose intake doors.
12.) Center wing access plate.
13.) Crew entrance door.
14.) Forward main landing gear doors.
15.) Bomb bay doors.
16.) Aft landing gear doors.
17.) Elevator stop adjustment access door.
18.) Elevator hinge access plate.
19.) Elevator tab push-pull rod.

ACCESS PLATE CALLOUTS, TOP VIEW:

1.) Access plate for leading edge removal.
2.) Elevator tab push-pull rod access plate.
3.) Anti-icing and electrical disconect access plates.
4.) Aft bomb bay tank fuel filler door.
5.) Fuel tank number four vent line and gage access plate.
6.) Number four fuel tank filler door.
7.) Number three fuel tank access plate.
8.) Wing fuel tank filler door.
9.) Anti-icing line and anti-icing shut-off valve actuator disconnects for engine removal.
10.) Access plate for aft engine section.
11.) Spoiler aileron air spring plate access plate.
12.) Constant level valve access plate.
13.) Wing tank vent line access plate.
14.) Number three fuel tank constant level and fuel gage unit access plate.
15.) Number two fuel tank filler door.
16.) Number two fuel tank access plate.
17.) Number one fuel tank access plate.
18.) Number one fuel tank filler door.
19.) Filler door for forward bomb bay fuel tank.
20.) Pilot's escape hatch.
21.) Co-pilot's escape hatch.
22.) Number one fuel tank vent line and fuel gage unit access plate.
23.) Number one fuel tank constant level access plate.
24.) Constant level valve access plate.
25.) Number two fuel tank vent line and gage unit access plate.
26.) Number three fuel tank vent line and gage unit access plate.
27.) Anti-icing fuel and hydraulic line access plates.
28.) Hydraulic suction line access plates.
29.) Access plates for leading edge anti-icing disconnects.
30.) Engine hoist attachment access plates.
31.) Removable leading edge.
32.) Vane drive linkage access plates (26).
33.) Wing tip light access cover.
34.) Vane torque tube drive access plates (14).
35.) Spoiler air spring, feel aileron cables, flap drive worm and track access plate.
36.) Spoiler aileron air spring inspection.
37.) Spoiler aileron bolt access plate.
38.) Spoiler aileron valve and cam adjustment access plate.
39.) Spoiler aileron cylinder, valve and quadrant access plate.
40.) Flap cable and drive inspection plate.
41.) Number three fuel tank filler door.
42.) Constant level valve access plate.
43.) Number four fuel tank constant level access plate.
44.) Number four fuel tank access plate.

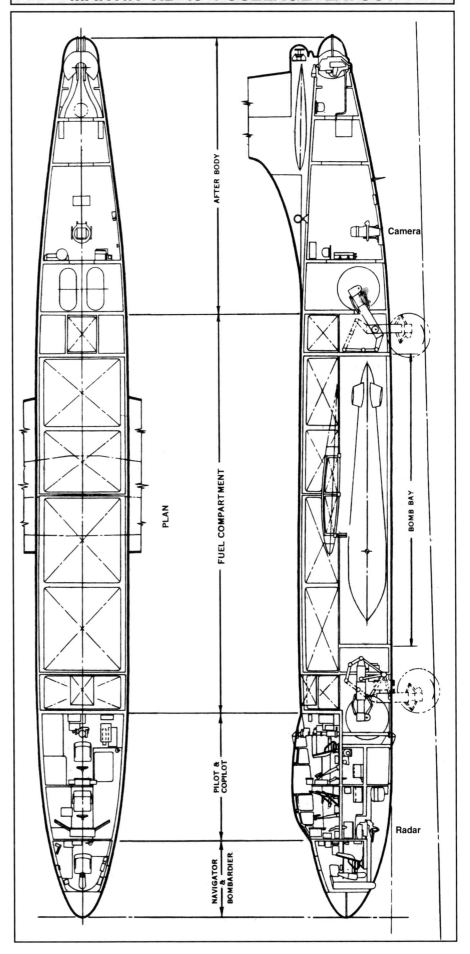

MARTIN XB-48 FUSELAGE LAYOUT

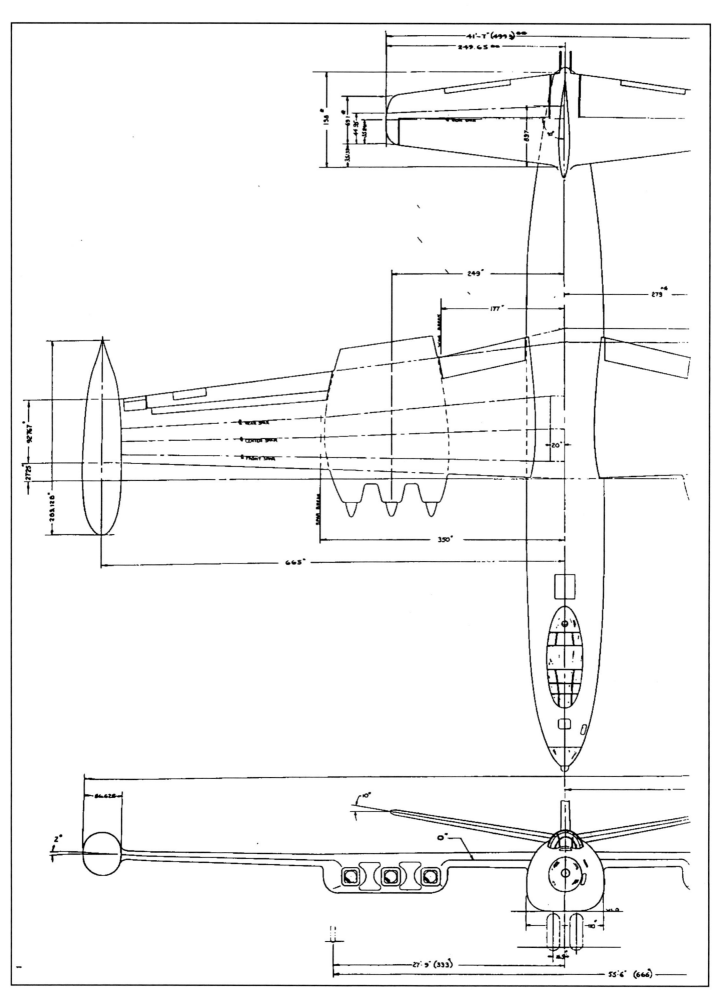

6

STATION DIAGRAMS

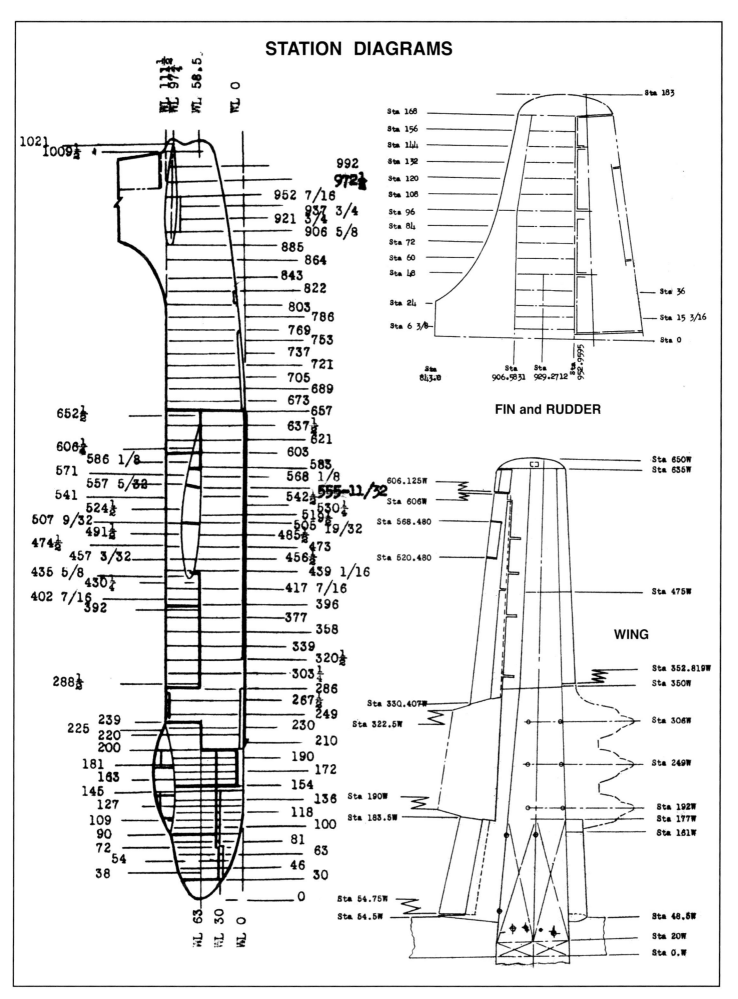

FIN and RUDDER

WING

MARTIN XB-48 MEDIUM BOMBER FLIGHT DECK CONFIGURATION

The forward pressurized section of the fuselage (station 0 to station 239) accomodated a crew of three consisting of the following:

Pilot:
Flight Controls
Engine Starting and Operations
Partial Radio Operations

Co-Pilot:
Radio Operations
Tail Gun Operation

Bombardier/Navigator:
Bomb Dropping Operations
Navigation
Radar Operation

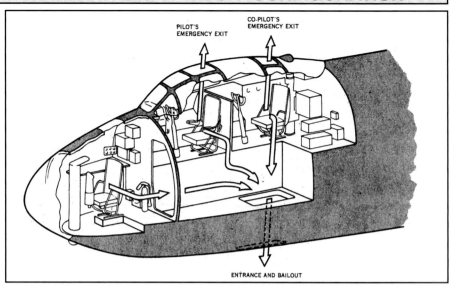

All fuselage sections from station 239 aft were unpressurized and there were no provisions for crew movement from the flight deck to the aft sections while in flight. The center fuselage section contained the bomb bay with fuselage fuel tanks above it. The aft fuselage section accomodated the tail gun turret, ammunition, and a remotely controlled camera.

FLIGHT DECK CALLOUTS
100.)	Y-2 Periscope
101.)	Indicator ID-218/APS-23
102.)	Control Box
103.)	Radar Control Box
104.)	Navigation Control
105.)	Ballistics Control
106.)	Stabilization Amplifier
107.)	Fire Extinguisher
108.)	Heading Unit
109.)	Navigation Table
110,)	Bombardier's Switch Panel
111.)	Navigator's Instruments
112.)	Selector Racks
113.)	Tracking Control
114.)	Stabilization Unit
115.)	True Air Speed Indicator
116.)	Heading Repeater
117.)	Time-To-Go Indicator
118.)	Bomb Release Control
119.)	Bombardier/Navigator Seat
120.)	Synchronizer SN-47/APS-23
121.)	Indicator Junction Box
122.)	Pilot's Rudder Pedals
123.)	Pilot's Instrument Panel
124.)	A-16 Compass
125.)	Pilot's Control Column
126.)	Pilot's Seat
127.)	Computer Amplifier AM(XA-191)/APA-59
128.)	Pilot's Oxygen Bottle
129.)	Power Supply PP(XA-40)/APA-59
130.)	Coordinate Converter ARM-1404
131.)	Pilot's Console
132.)	Pilot's Oxygen Regulator
133.)	Co-Pilot's Rudder Pedals
134.)	C0-Pilot's Console
135.)	Co-Pilot's Instrument Panel
136.)	Co-Pilot's Control Column

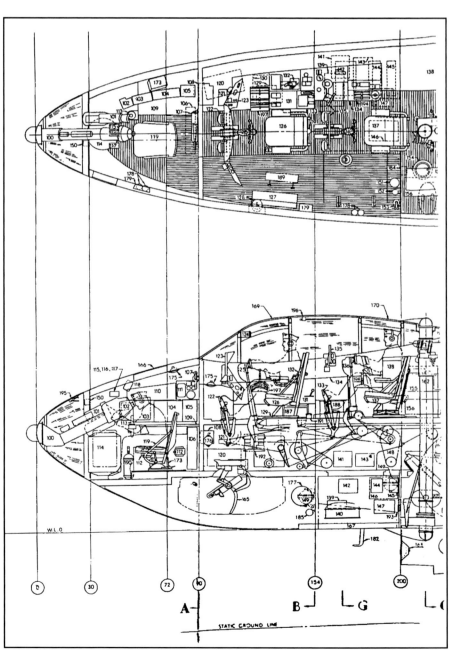

137.) Co-Pilot's Seat
138.) Electrical Distribution Panel
139.) Meter Unit MP(XA-120)/APA-59
140.) Transmitter Receiver
141.) Roll Computer
142.) Synchronizer SN(XA-9)/APQ-31
143.) Rectifier Power Unit
144.) Servo Amplifier AM-193/APA-23
145.) Power Supply PP(XA-41)/AP2-31
146.) Battery Box
147.) Power Supply PP(XA-40)/APA-59
148.) Cabin Pressure Regulator
149.) Emergency Hydraulic Accumulator
150.) Inclinometer
151.) Drinking Water Container
152.) Cup Holder
153.) Fire Extinguisher
154.) Supercharging Safety Valve
155.) Liaison Transmitter/Crystal Unit
156.) Liaison Receiver/Dynamotor
157.) Interphone Mixer Amplifier
158.) Guide Path Receiver
159.) Interphone Amplifier
160.) Localizer Receiver/Dynamotor
161.) Interphone Relay Unit
162.) Farrano Sight
163.) Modulator
164.) Air Conditioner
165.) Antenna AS-34/APS-23
166.) Navigator's Sighting Window
167.) Entrance Door
168.) Landing Light
169.) Pilot's Escape Hatch
170.) Co-Pilot's Escape Hatch
171.) Emergency Life Raft Release Handle
172.) C0-Pilot's Oxygen Bottle
173.) A-2 Bombing Timer
174.) Fuel Level Adjustment Box
175.) Dome Light
176.) Nose Wheel Steering Accumulator
177.) Emergency Hydraulic Reservoir
178.) Relief Containers
179.) First Aid Kit
180.) Emergency Brake Bottle
181.) Emergency Bomb Door Bottle
182.) Pitot Tube
183.) Voltage Regulator Housing
184.) Switch Box
185.) Main Emergency Pump Unit (Hyd)
186.) Liaison Antenna
187.) Pilot's Data Case
188.) Co-Pilot's Data Case
189.) Fuel Selector Switch Panel
190.) Navigator's Oxygen Bottle
191.) Landing Gear Warning Horn
192.) Throttle Power Boost Packages
193.) Bomb Bay Door Safety Latch
194.) Co-Pilot's Pedestal
195.) AN/ARN-5 Glide Path Antenna
196.) RC-103 Localizer Antenna
197.) Pilot's Pedestal

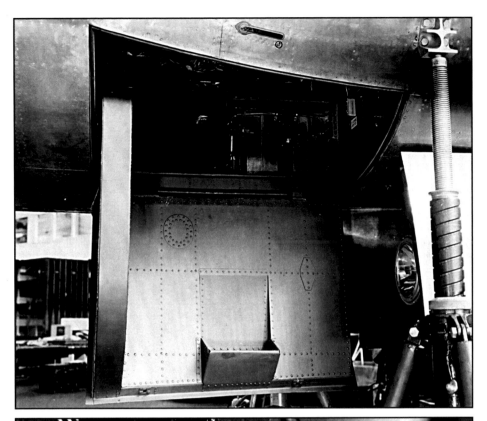

At top right, open crew entry and escape hatch viewed from the left side of the fuselage. (NARA via Bill Spidle) At right, access to the co-pilot's position with interior crew entry and exit hatch opened vertically at right. (NARA via Bill Spidle)

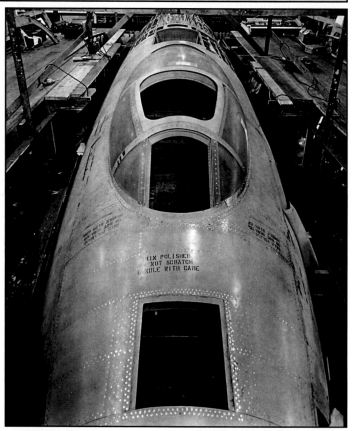

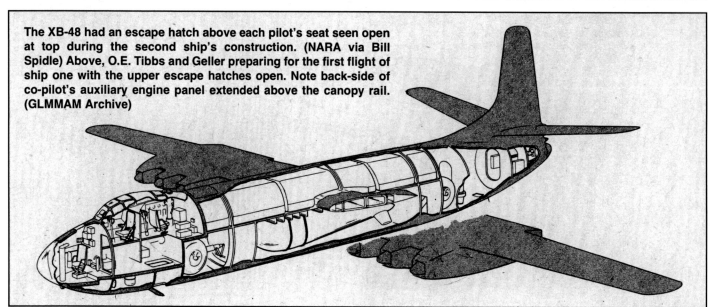

The XB-48 had an escape hatch above each pilot's seat seen open at top during the second ship's construction. (NARA via Bill Spidle) Above, O.E. Tibbs and Geller preparing for the first flight of ship one with the upper escape hatches open. Note back-side of co-pilot's auxiliary engine panel extended above the canopy rail. (GLMMAM Archive)

XB-48 PILOT'S RIGHT-HAND COCKPIT THROTTLE PANEL

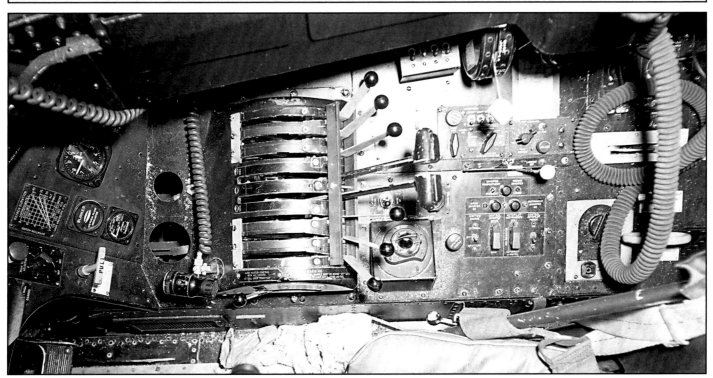

At left, co-pilot's instrument panel as seen on the XB-48 mock-up. (NARA via Bill Spidle)

Bottom, co-pilot's instrument panel on 23 July 1947 as flown in ship one. Main panel legend: left-to-right top row; clock, airspeed indicator, directional indicator and vertical gyro. Bottom row: left-to-right; trim tab indicator, rate-of-climb indicator, turn-and-bank indicator, altimeter, and unused. A twelve gauge engine instument panel was added on the right of the main panel. It could be used to monitor each wing's three engines at one time and could be switched between the two wings. The three instruments accross the bottom were for oil temperatures. The top three gauges on the left were tachometers. The top three in the center monitered fuel pressure and the top three on the right captured tail pipe temperatures. (GLMMAM Archive)

Co-Pilot's Meter Panel Legend:
1.) Light
2.) Voltmeter Selector Switch
3.) Amp Meters
4.) Generator Switches
5.) Battery Switch
6.) Voltage Test Jacks
7.) Voltmeter

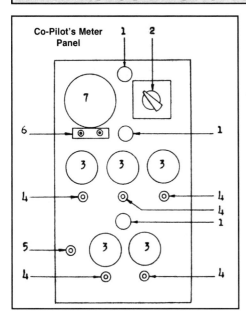

Co-Pilot's Meter Panel

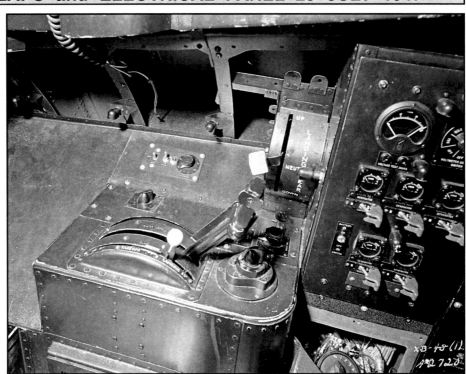

At right, co-pilot's flap control quadrant. Below, co-pilot's meter panel and circuit breaker panel. (GLMMAM Archive)

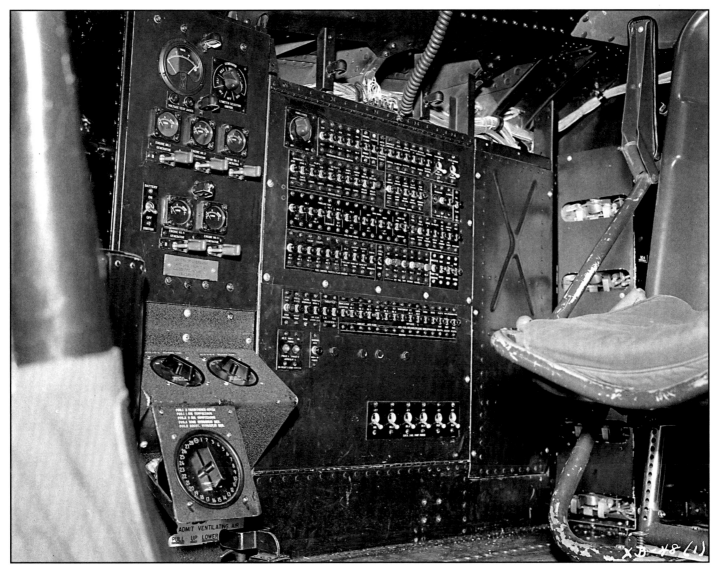

XB-48 mock-up bombardier/navigator compartment on 21 May 1945. Above left, left side of compartment looking forward. The pipe-like structure represented the Y-2 periscope (NARA via Bill Spidle) Above right, right side of co-pilot's station looking forward with ID-218/APS-23 indicator at left. (NARA via Bill Spidle) Below, bomb bay armament panels located on the left fuselage side of the mock-up. (NARA via Bill Spidle) At right, mock-up aft bulkhead of the bombardier/navigator compartment with access tunnel at the right. (NARA via Bill Spidle)

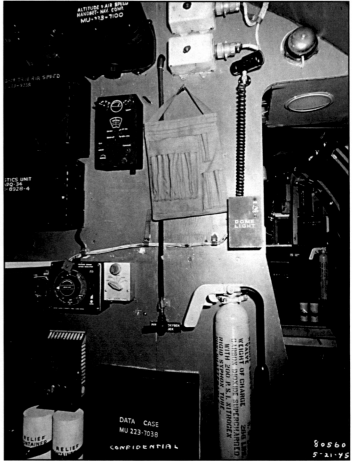

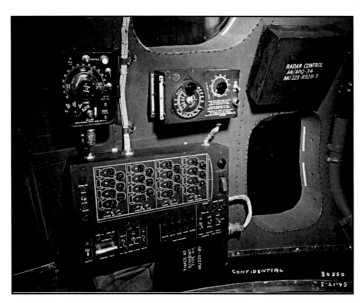

On the right side of the fuselage above the navigator's table was a small panel containing four gauges as seen at right and bottom. These gauges were:

1.) Airspeed Indicator
2.) Repeater Direction Indicator
3.) Clock
4.) Altimeter

Below, bombardier / navigator's station on ship one on 8 April 1947. (NARA via Bill Spidel)

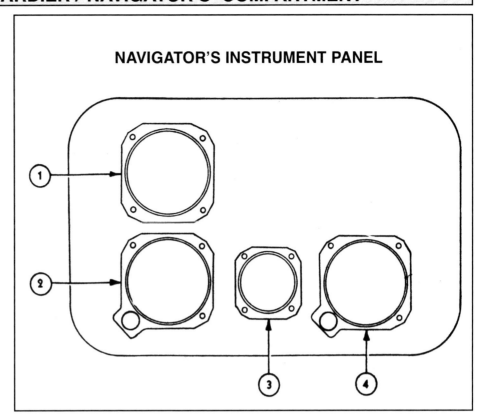

NAVIGATOR'S INSTRUMENT PANEL

A-598
4-8-47

MARTIN'S UNIQUE XB-48 TANDEM LANDING GEAR with OUTRIGGERS

With performance and bomb load in mind, Martin developed the XB-48's tandem landing gear with outriggers to allow for a high performance thin wing and a continuous bomb bay for carrying very large bombs at the center of gravity of the airplane. This type gear proved so successful that it was used on both the Boeing B-47 medium bomber and the Boeing B-52 heavy bomber as well as the innovative Martin XB-51 (see Air Force Legends #201) .

During design development, Martin fitted tandem gear to a B-26, designated XB-26H, as a proof-of-concept test ship. This aircraft, S/N 44-68221, was nicknamed the "The Middle River Stump Jumper".

The XB-48 highly efficient and rather unique landing gear arrangement consisted of two main gears with dual wheels and brakes mounted in tandem and retracting entirely within the fuselage contour. The forward gear was arranged to retract forward while the rear gear retracted aft, thus resulting in a negligible center-of-gravity (c.g.) when extending or retracting the gear. The front wheels were steerable and was operated by toe pedals on the pilot's and co-pilot's rudder control pedals replacing the usual brake pedals. The brakes were operated by a hand control located on the pilot's and co-pilot's control wheels.

For lateral stability on the ground, small auxiliary wheels were mounted on each side at approximately the semi-span of the wing. These then would retract forward into the outboard engine nacelles. These stabilizing wheels were full-swiveling (360°) and, therefore, took no side load. All side load was carried by the main tandem gear.

Above and below, XB-26H "The Middle River Stump Jumper", S/N 44-68221, at Martin 20 January 1947. (GLMMAM Archive)

MARTIN XB-48 OUTRIGGER LANDING GEAR

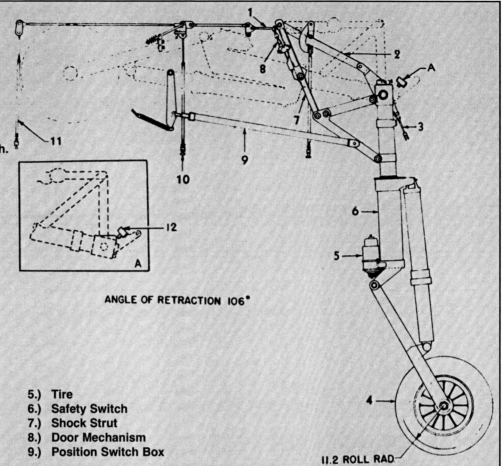

OUTRIGGER LANDING GEAR
1.) Door Latch Installation
2.) Hydraulic Retracting Cyl.
3.) Aft Door Operating Mech.
4.) Tire
5.) Shimmy Damper
6.) Shock Strut
7.) Strut
8.) Switch Installation
9.) Forward Door Operating Mech.
10.) Locks Installation
11.) Door Latch Installation
12.) Position Switch Box

FRONT MAIN GEAR
1.) Drag Strut
2.) Drag Strut Switch
3.) Diagonal Brace
4.) Position Switch
5.) Fulorum Truss
6.) Steering Cylinder
7.) Shock Strut
8.) Tire
9.) Steer Position Indicator Transmitter

AFT MAIN GEAR
1.) Hydraulic Cylinder
2.) Strut
3.) Switch
4.) Brake Lines
5.) Tire
6.) Safety Switch
7.) Shock Strut
8.) Door Mechanism
9.) Position Switch Box

ANGLE OF RETRACTION 106°

11.2 ROLL RAD

FRONT MAIN GEAR

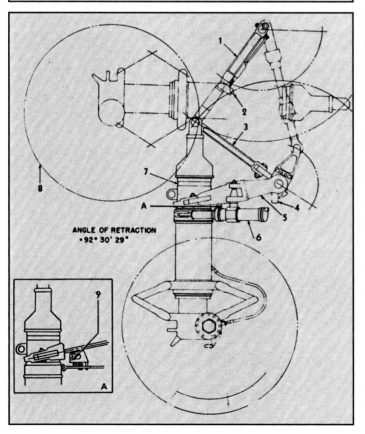

ANGLE OF RETRACTION
•92° 30' 29"

AFT MAIN GEAR

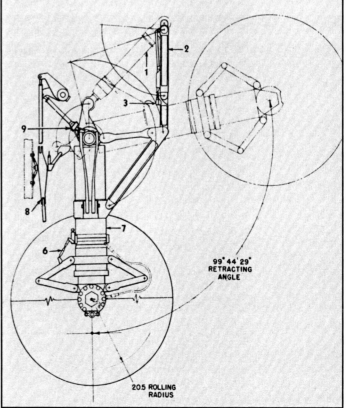

99° 44' 29"
RETRACTING
ANGLE

20.5 ROLLING
RADIUS

17

Above left, left outrigger gear. Above right, front view of left gear. Below, left outrigger gear ship two. (NARA vis Bill Spidle)

Above, head-on view of front main gear with landing lights mounted on each gear door. (Craig Kaston collection) At right, aft view of rear main gear without tires and wheels attached. (GLMMAM Archive) Below right, same view with tires and rims attached. Note smooth flat surface of thick landing gear doors. (GLMMAM Archive) Below, nose gear struts and axles prior to installation. (GLMMAM Archive)

Above, completed nose gear doors on the factory floor. Below, ship two with tow bar on nose gear. (both GLMMAM Archive)

Above, left-hand view of ship one showing nose wheel and open entry/bail out door. (GLMMAM Archive) Below, right-hand view of nose wheel and door on ship two on 1 February 1949. Engine trim and logo was black. (GLMMAM Archive)

XB-48 HORIZONTAL BOMB BAY

The horizontal type bomb bay developed for the XB-48 deserves special mention because of the variety of bombs accommodated and the simplicity of loading. This arrangement permitted a multiplicity of bomb loading arrangements ranging from 36-250lb bombs to one 22,000lb "Grand Slam" bomb. Up to four Martin designed bomb carriers were used, which could hold from one to nine bombs depending on size from 250lb through 1,000lb. Two larger carriers were used to carry 1,600lb and 2,000lb bombs. Standard Army bomb racks were integrated with the Martin designed bomb carriers. These Martin carriers permitted from one to nine bombs to be shackled, chocked, and fused on the ground. The loaded carriers were then hoisted and latched into the bomb bay in one operation, thus reducing the actual bomb loading time to a minimum. All bombs, bomb carriers, and bomb bay fuel tanks were hoisted by using two 12,000lb Army electrically driven chain hoists.

The bomb bay doors were pneumatically operated and could be opened and closed in two seconds thus permitting the airplane to fly in the "clean" condition during most of the bombing run. The doors were designed to retract entirely within the fuselage contour, thus reducing drag to a minimum when the doors were operated for releasing bombs. A special switch, accessible from outside the airplane, was provided for opening the bomb bay doors on the ground. This switch made it unnecessary to enter the airplane in order to open the doors and also prevented closing the doors on the bomb-loading crew, or the accidental release of bombs during the loading process.

BOMB BAY MOCK-UP 24 MAY 1945

Above, mock-up bomb bay with 18-500lb bombs and aft auxiliary fuel tank. Below left, 18-500lb bombs. Below, 22,000lb "Grand Slam" bomb. (all NARA via Bill Spidle)

The Martin designed bomb carriers ("A" carriers) could hold a maximum of nine 250 or 500 lb bombs arranged in three rows. The first row or layer consisted of four bombs attached to the "A" carrier. This was accomplished by using eight "U" hook adapters which were attached to the forward and aft end of the 14-inch Army S-2 bomb rack and in turn latched to the carrier. The second layer consisted of three bombs, which were mounted under the first layer bombs. Three adjustable screw type suspension rods were attached to the S-2 bomb rack. The bombs were latched to the S-2 bomb rack and in turn the suspension rod was mounted on the "A" carrier. The third layer consisted of two bombs which were attached to the center second layer bomb by means of the auxiliary shackle. The three suspension rods were then tightened until the side motion was eliminated and all bombs nested closely together.

Three bombs could be attached to the "A" carrier in reverse layering. One bomb would be attached to an Army S-1 bomb shackle attached to the "A" carrier. This bomb would then be fitted with an auxiliary bomb release shackle M-223 that would support two bombs in a second layer.

Above, 3-500 lb bombs slung with an S-1 and M-223 bomb shackles. (NARA via Bill Spid) Below, XB-48 bomb bay in ship two. (GLMMAM Archive)

NINE - PLACE MARTIN TYPE "A" BOMB CARRIER

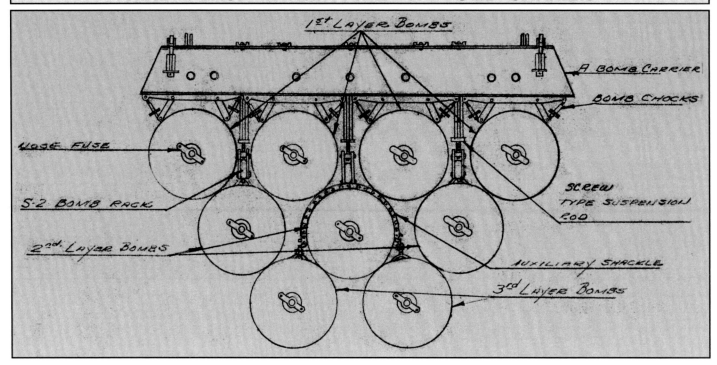

Below, fully loaded Martin Type "A" bomb carrier with nine 500 lb bombs on 24 November 1946 during drop tests. (NARA)

XB-48 BOMB LOADS

LOAD	WEIGHT	DESIGNATION	TOTAL WEIGHT
36	250 lbs	AN-M57A1	9,000 lbs
36	500 lbs	AN-M64A1	18,000 lbs
36	500 lbs	AN-M58	18,000 lbs
10	1,000 lbs	AN-M65A1	10,000 lbs
10	1,000 lbs	AN-M59	10,000 lbs
14	1,000 lbs	AN-M33	14,000 lbs
8	1,600 lbs	AN-M1	12,800 lbs
6	2,000 lbs	AN-M66	12,000 lbs
2	4,000 lbs	AN-M56A1	8,000 lbs
1	10,000 lbs	T1	10,000 lbs
1	12,000 lbs	"Tall Boy"	12,000 lbs
1	22,000 lbs	"Grand Slam"	22,000 lbs
2	570 gal	Fuel Tank	7,528 lbs

2000-Pound G.P. Bombs—6
Total Weight 12,000 Pounds

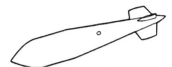

22,000-Pound "Grand Slam"—1
Total Weight 22,000 Pounds

250-Pound G.P. Bombs—36
Total Weight 9,000 Pounds

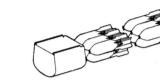

1000-Pound Demolition Bombs—10
500 Gal. Aux. Fuel Tanks—2
Total Weight 17,528 Pounds

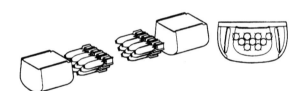

250-Pound G.P. Bombs—18
500 Gal. Aux. Fuel Tanks—2
Total Weight 12,028. Pounds

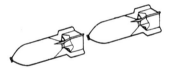

4000-Pound L.C. Bombs—2
Total Weight 8,000 Pounds

500-Pound G.P. Bombs—36
Total Weight 18,000 Pounds

12,000-Pound "Tall Boy"—1
Total Weight 12,000 Pounds

1600-Pound A.P. Bombs—8
Total Weight 12,800 Pounds

500-Pound G.P. Bombs—18
500 Gal. Aux. Fuel Tanks—2
Total Weight 16,528 Pounds

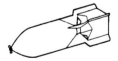

10,000 Pound Demolition Bomb—1
Total Weight 10,000 Pounds

The XB-48 tail turret which would have been operated by the co-pilot was originally planned as a Martin designed ball turret with a 50° arc in all quadrants. Instead, a streamlined inoperable XB-45 turret was installed. It also had a 100° cone of fire and was supplied with 600 rounds of ammunition. It also could be upgraded to two .60 caliber guns and 350 rounds of ammunition. Above, twin .50 caliber remote controlled tail turret displaying full left lateral defection. It was only fitted on ship two. (GLMMAM Archive) Below, tail turret in the standard trail position. (GLMMAM Archive)

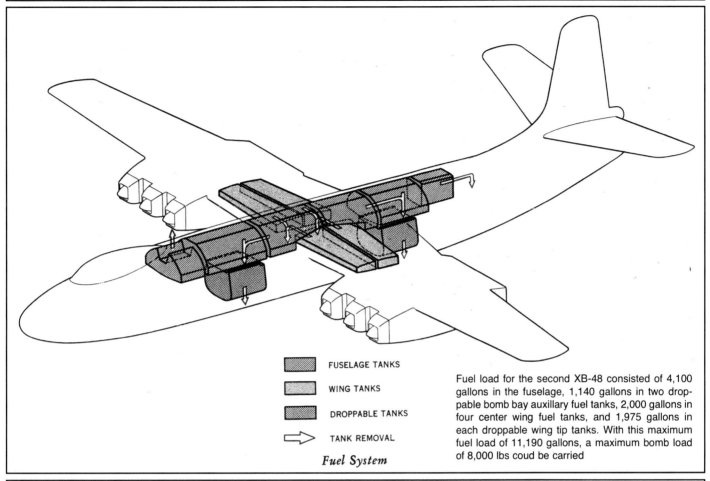

FUSELAGE TANKS

WING TANKS

DROPPABLE TANKS

TANK REMOVAL

Fuel System

Fuel load for the second XB-48 consisted of 4,100 gallons in the fuselage, 1,140 gallons in two droppable bomb bay auxillary fuel tanks, 2,000 gallons in four center wing fuel tanks, and 1,975 gallons in each droppable wing tip tanks. With this maximum fuel load of 11,190 gallons, a maximum bomb load of 8,000 lbs coud be carried

ALLISON BUILT GENERAL ELECTRIC TG-180/J35 ENGINES & NACELLES

The six 4,000 lb thrust J35 engines on the XB-48 were fitted into a unique set of engine nacelles. Martin design theory and wind tunnel data showed that divergence airflow drag could be reduced by as much as 10% by using by-pass ducts between fairly tight individual nacelles joined by a thin airfoil plate across the bottom of the three engines mounted under each wing. The Army Air Forces advised against it, but Martin produced the aircraft with the by-pass anyway. The ducts worked well at lower speeds, but at high speeds, air dammed up in front of the nacelles and limited the aircrafts top speed.

The engines had very short tailpipes with almost no rear fairings or shrouds. It looked like the rear of the nacelles were just forgotten by the engineers. The reality was they were adequately faired by airflow with little loss. Efficiency of the jet outlet was further improved by use of a controllable area tailpipe, of a type designed

to avoid hot-spots by permitting external cooling airflow.

Engine access and removal was relatively quick and easy. The leading edge air intake assembly, serving all three engines, was hinged to swing upward. Opening the leading edge provided access to the engine accessories and oil tanks. For access to the rear portions of the engines, hinged doors were arranged for easy handling after the leading edge had been raised. Access to the tailpipes was achieved by opening the landing flaps which extended across the nacelle at the trailing edge.

In order to remove the engines, jack screws were incorporated in the mounts which permitted the engines to be lowered onto rails upon which they could be moved forward to clear the flap supporting structure. Upon being moved forward, the engines could be removed either by being pushed forward onto a dolly or by

being lowered by a hoist to a supporting dolly or cradle.

The first XB-48 was fitted with J35-7 (TG-180-B1 engines that were plagued with fuel control problems, while the second ship was fitted with improved J35-9 (TG-180-C1) engines.

Below, the complicated fuel panel was stowed across the crawlway to the left of the pilot. It had to be pulled out and placed in position. (NARA)

XB-48 ENGINE NACELLES

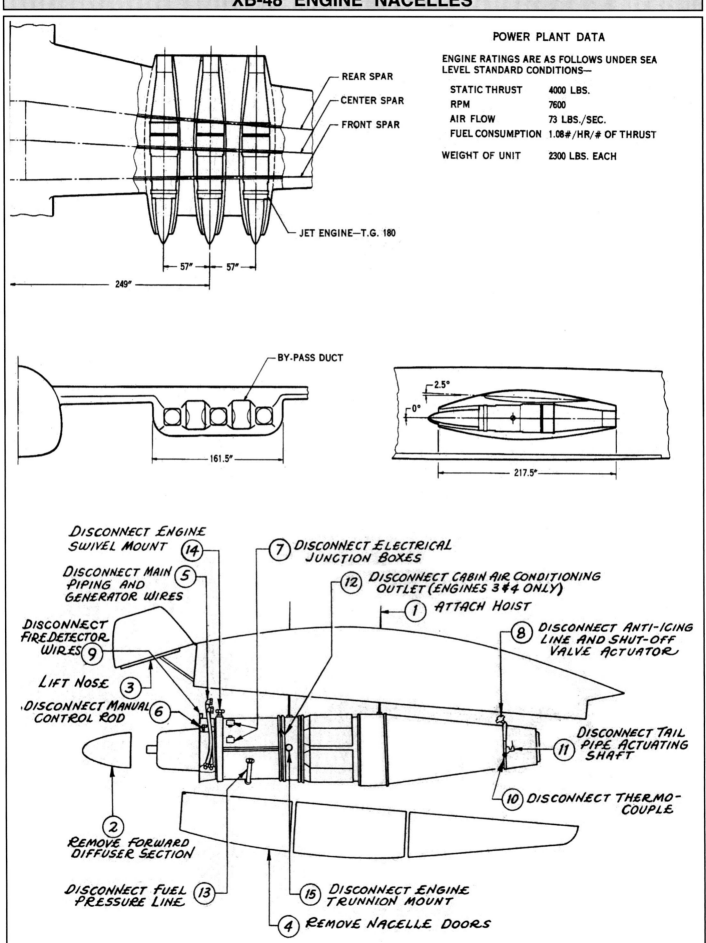

POWER PLANT DATA

ENGINE RATINGS ARE AS FOLLOWS UNDER SEA
LEVEL STANDARD CONDITIONS—

STATIC THRUST	4000 LBS.
RPM	7600
AIR FLOW	73 LBS./SEC.
FUEL CONSUMPTION	1.08#/HR/# OF THRUST
WEIGHT OF UNIT	2300 LBS. EACH

REAR SPAR
CENTER SPAR
FRONT SPAR

JET ENGINE—T.G. 180

57" 57"
249"

BY-PASS DUCT
161.5"

2.5°
0°
217.5"

DISCONNECT ENGINE SWIVEL MOUNT (14)

DISCONNECT ELECTRICAL JUNCTION BOXES (7)

DISCONNECT MAIN PIPING AND GENERATOR WIRES (5)

DISCONNECT CABIN AIR CONDITIONING OUTLET (ENGINES 3 & 4 ONLY) (12)

(1) ATTACH HOIST

DISCONNECT FIRE DETECTOR WIRES (9)

(8) DISCONNECT ANTI-ICING LINE AND SHUT-OFF VALVE ACTUATOR

LIFT NOSE (3)

DISCONNECT MANUAL CONTROL ROD (6)

(11) DISCONNECT TAIL PIPE ACTUATING SHAFT

(10) DISCONNECT THERMO-COUPLE

(2) REMOVE FORWARD DIFFUSER SECTION

DISCONNECT FUEL PRESSURE LINE (13)

(15) DISCONNECT ENGINE TRUNNION MOUNT

(4) REMOVE NACELLE DOORS

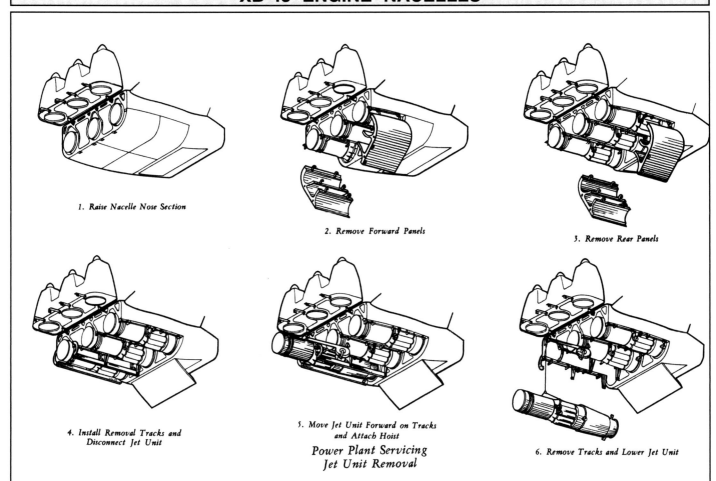

1. Raise Nacelle Nose Section

2. Remove Forward Panels

3. Remove Rear Panels

4. Install Removal Tracks and Disconnect Jet Unit

5. Move Jet Unit Forward on Tracks and Attach Hoist

*Power Plant Servicing
Jet Unit Removal*

6. Remove Tracks and Lower Jet Unit

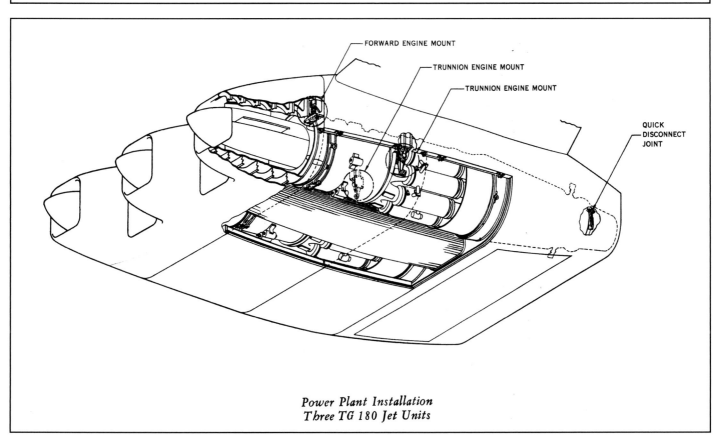

FORWARD ENGINE MOUNT

TRUNNION ENGINE MOUNT

TRUNNION ENGINE MOUNT

QUICK DISCONNECT JOINT

*Power Plant Installation
Three TG 180 Jet Units*

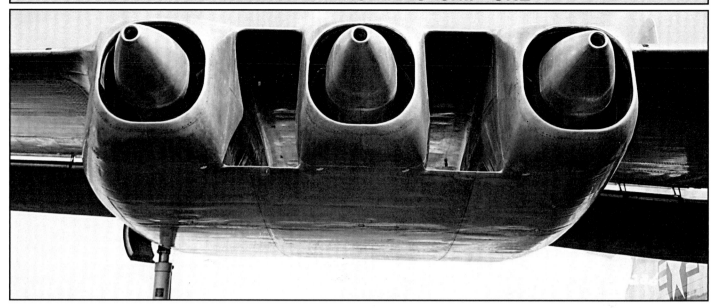

Above, right wing intakes and by-pass ducts on the first XB-48. (NARA via Bill Spidle) Below, unfaired engine exhausts with a clear view through the by-pass ducts. (GLMMAM Archive) Bottom, outside view of right outer engine nacelle on the first XB-48. (GLMMAM Archive)

Above, by-pass ducts on ship 2 on 20 July 1948. Below, black intake trim on ship two were actually anti-icing blankets. (GLM-MAM Archive)

Above and below, engine installation on ship one on 6 March 1947. Note raised intakes. Below, left-to-right: George Harris, Frank Buckley, and William LeBrun. (GLMMAM Archive)

Mock-up inspection was held on 19 April 1945, after which work started in earnest. On 27 August 1945, the designed wing area of the XB-48 was increased by 226 sq.ft. to shorten its take off distance.

Due in large part to supply chain problems for materials and GFE (Government Furnished Equipment), progress was slow and in February 1946 the AMC (Air Material Command) warned Martin it could lose its contract if things did not change. This forced Martin to make two corrections to the program. The first was to reorganize the project to basically mirror Lockheed's "Skunk Works" management operation of the F-80 program. The second was to solicit the Army to allow Martin to make material substitutions on the first ship in order to meet the target dates. Since such substitutions would undoubtedly add weight to the aircraft, it was promised that the second

ship would utilize correct materials and be re-engineered to be within contract weights so that tactical tests could be accomplished. Because of this, ship one was some 14,000 lbs overweight when it accomplished its first flight. The re-engineering of the second ship was successful as it came in 95 lbs underweight. However, changes in GFE over which Martin had no control resulted in the second XB-48 being 2,000 lbs overweight.

By 1 January 1947, with 253 people working on the first ship, all its basic engineering had been completed and 29,680 engineering detail orders had been released for manufacturing. The total number of drafting hours spent on ship one since the project started was 171,335 hours. All the engineering remaining to be done on ship one was: testing (static, laboratory, vibration etc.), liaison, development items (such as tubing, conduit runs, cockpit lighting, etc.), reports and miscellaneous items.

Tool design was 100% complete on all major components as were all major assembly fixtures. In addition, all tools were completed. However, Martin was still delayed while waiting for nineteen different GFE pieces of equipment. In addition, Martin was also waiting on five subcontractors for parts. They were waiting on Curtiss Wright for reworked landing gear expected by 25 January, a left-hand landing gear cylinder expected on 10 January, and a sequence valve for the forward landing gear expected on 8 January. Additionally, Westinghouse owed them a replacement air compressor and cylinder for the

Below, final assembly of ship one in Building E on 8 March 1947. (GLMMAM Archive)

Above, right wing inner (center) and outer flaps in full down position with the long outer upper wing aileron spoiler extended on 3 March 1947. (NARA vis Bill Spidle) Below, ship one under construction on 8 March 1947. (GLMMAM Archive)

pneumatic system. Lastly, a new fin tip was expected to be delivered on 25 January to replace the plastic ground test only tip on ship one.

As 1947 started, Martin's work was mostly centered around the completion of the flight controls. These were the: rudder, fin, leading edge of fin, center wing flaps, outer wing flaps, stabilizer, leading edge of stabilizer, aft landing gear installation, front landing gear installation and right wing engine nacelle underside.

On 26 February 1947, the Army notified Martin that ship one would receive TG-180-B-1/J35-7 engines and ship two would receive TG-180-C-1/J35-9 engines. It was decided that ship one would be completed

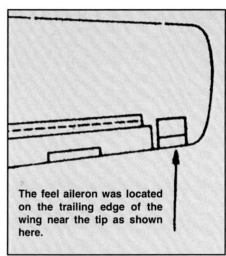

The feel aileron was located on the trailing edge of the wing near the tip as shown here.

XB-48 S/N 45-59585 ROLL OUT, 11 APRIL 1947

without an operational bombardier/ navigator station or a tail turret. Mostly due to delays in GFE parts including engines, the roll out was delayed until 11 April 1947.

On 11 April 1947, S/N 45-59585 was rolled out of the assembly hangar for its public display and then towed down Wilson Road to the Martin airport in preparation for its first flight. (GLMMAM Archive)

Above, S/N 45-59585 being towed out on 11 April 1947. (GLMMAM Archive) Below, Left-to-right: William Eager, Capt. J. Colopy, Major Auston Speed, Wing Commander H. Connaghan, BGEN Franklin Carroll, Roy Shoults, Air Marshall George Jones, and Capt. W. Ranny inspect 585 on 11 April 1947. (GLMMAM Archive)

On 11 April 1947, S/N 45-59585 was rolled out of the hangar and towed down Wilson Road to the Martin airport. (GLMMAM)

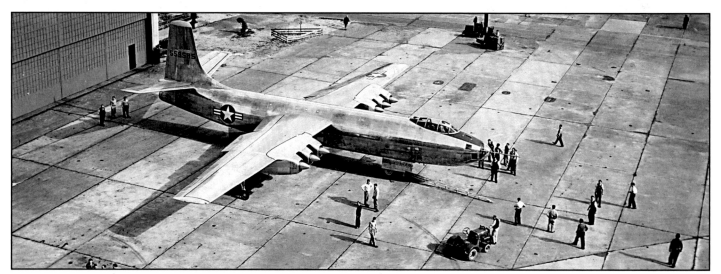

38

Above, Martin flight line with production AM-1, XB-48, prototype Mauler and a PBM-5A Mariner in April 1947. (NARA via Bill Spidle) Below, two views of ship one being prepped for its first flight on 10 July 1947. It was a failed attempt as one of the outrigger gears was damaged and the first flight was delayed for repairs. (GLMMAM Archive)

SHIP ONE'S FIRST FLIGHT, 22 JUNE 1947

On 17 June 1947, Martin's Director of Flight R.E. "Pat" Tibbs attempted to make the XB-48's first flight with E.R. Gelvin as co-pilot. As Tibbs turned onto the take-off runway one of the outrigger gear collapsed and the flight was cancelled. Five days later, on 22 June 1947, after repairs were made, a successful first flight was made. Three months earlier on 24 March 1947, the Army and Martin agreed to transfer flight testing to the Naval Air Test Center, NAS Patuxent River, MD, because its runways were twice the length of the 5,500 ft runway at Martin. So at 5:55 am Tibbs and Gelvin took off for a 37 minute, 73 mile flight over Chesapeake Bay to Patuxent River. The flight was uneventful but the landing was marred. The oversensitive hand braking system locked up and two of the main gear tires blew.

The following day, on 23 June, GEN Craigie telegrammed Mr. Martin to congratulate Martin and his company on the success of the XB-48's first flight. After this first flight, E.R. Gelvin, became the Martin XB-48 test pilot.

Martin's Director of Flight R.E. "Pat' Tibbs (at right) prior to the XB-48's first flight attempt on 17 June 1947 accompanied by E.R. Gelvin (center). George Pitcher is on the left. A collapsed outrigger gear postponed the first flight until 22 June. (GLMMAM Archive) Below, ship one taxis-out for its first flight. (GLMMAM Archive)

Above, first XB-48 flight on 22 June 1947 was made by "Pat" Tibbs, all others were piloted by Martin's test pilot E.R. Gelvin. (GLMMAM Archive) At right, gear retraction on S/N 45-59585. The aft main gear is fully retracted and the gear doors are almost closed, forward main gear is about 50% retracted and outrigger is rotating slowly forward into the engine nacelles. (GLM-MAM Archive) Below, ship one landing on the 11,000 ft runway at NAS Patuxent River, MD, just 73 miles from the Martin factory. (GLMMAM Archive) Bottom, aircraft at the Naval Air Test Center (NATC) Patuxent River, MD, late on 22 June 1947 after its blown tires were replaced. (USN)

FLIGHT 16 TAKE - OFF ACCIDENT, 21 NOVEMBER 1947

Phase One testing was stalled for several weeks beginning on 21 November 1947, when ship one experienced a take-off accident during flight 16. During the pre-flight checks it was noted that the #5 fire warning light flickered several times, which was not unusual for these engines while warming up. The light went off and the engines were advanced to take-off rpm. The attempted take-off time was 7:49 am from runway 13. E.R. Gelvin started his take-off run at a gross weight of 98,500 lbs and a center-of-gravity of 25%. Observers stated that the front left main wheel and possibly the left rear main wheel started smoking shortly after the take-off roll started. This was followed by the #5 engine fire warning light at 4,000 ft of roll. With 7,000 ft of runway left, Gelvin elected to abort. When he applied the brakes the aircraft's progress did not slow and the pneumatic pressure had dropped from 1,300 lbs to 500 lbs. He then pulled the emergency brake lever and the ship slowed momentarily then continued as if it had no brakes. He attempted to retrack the gear and when that failed steered off the runway and slid to a stop. After crash inspection showed no engine fire. The cause of the accident was a break in the expander tube of the right forward wheel outboard brake.

Above and below, two views of ship one after its take-off accident at NAS Patuxent River, MD, on 21 November 1947. (NARA via Bill Spidle) Bottom, after landing at Martin, "Dutch" Gelvin (still in parachute), was surprised with an engine fire after shutdown on 20 July 1948. Damage was minimal as the aircraft was ferried to Wright Field on 24 July 1948. (GLMMAM Archive)

ENGINE FIRE, 20 JULY 1948

The flight test program of the XB-48 was to be conducted by phases. Phase One consisted of flying the first airplane approximately 30 hours. This phase was to be conducted by the contractor to determine whether the airplane would meet the performance guarantees. The Army would conduct Phase Two testing, which consisted of preliminary evaluation and performance checks. Any deficiences found would be corrected in ship two. All Phase One testing was conducted at the Patuxent NAS.

Martin expected ship one to be ready for flight tests by January 1947. However, Phase One testing actually got underway on 22 June 1947 with 45-59585's first flight. Phase One testing was to be completed in November 1947, but was delayed to May 1948 due to a crash, GFE engine issues, hydraulic contamination and other flight test problems. During Phase One testing Martin pilots tested ship one on 52 flights, for a total flight time of 41 hours

In addition to the lack of bombing gear in the nose compartment on ship one, the bomb bay was only partially functional with a maximum capacity of two bombs.

In late July/early August 1947, the test program on ship one was delayed for three weeks because the test stand hydraulic pumps disintegrated which resulted in both main hydraulic and boost systems being filled with chips of metal from the pumps.

The J35-7-B-1 engines fitted in ship one were plagued by fuel control problems so much so that the "master throttle" was virtually useless. Each throttle had to be adjusted individually through minute adjustments and the engines were prone to compressor stalls. To correct the problem, Martin was instructed on 22 September 1947 to investigate the feasibility of

Above, after the take-off accident ship one is seen landing back at Martin for repairs and upgrades including the large Martin XB-48 lettering seen below as it takes off once again. (GLM-MAM Archive)

installing J33 controls on all its J35-7 engines on the airplane and stored as spares. On 22 December, Martin responded that the proposed modification would cost $10,517.03 to convert the six XB-48 engines and airframe and another $4,899.76 to update the eight GFE engines held in reserve. As the J35-C-1 engines slated for ship two would pretty much solve the problem, the change was not initially made.

Also on 22 December, Martin proposed a $935.85 fix to eliminate a possible fire hazard. The fix was to prevent the gear case from flooding with regulator leakage oil when the

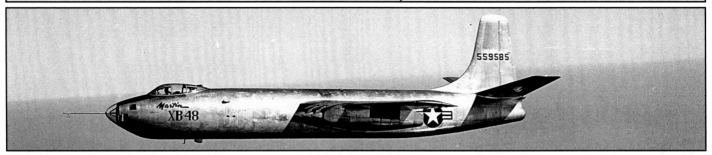

Above, ship one at right and ship two at left on 24 July 1948. At right, delivery of ship one to the Army was conducted by Martin test pilots E.R. Gelvin (far left) and Frank Christofferson (far right). Army pilots Claire Whitney (left middle) and Russ Schleeh (right middle) are seen here on 24 July 1948. Bottom, the aircraft was flown to Patuxent River, refueled, then delivered to Wright Field on 25 July. Bottom, ship one being pushed out in preparation for its ferry flight on 24 July. (all GLMMAM Archive)

J35-7-B-1 engine was shut off, but still windmilling.

On 3 February 1948, Martin was told to install the J33 controls on the aircraft's engines and the seven spares still in storage. By the time Phase I testing of ship one was completed, the aircraft had used fourteen -7 engines.

Flight testing had discovered a condition it named as right spoiler jump and on 9 February 1948 the liaison officer notified the Army that the XB-48 could not be flown at a reasonably high Mach number. The condition was finally corrected in late March.

Considerable delay was encountered in getting Phase Two test underway. According to the Flight Test Division, a major cause of the delay resulted from unsatisfactory instrumentation work accomplished by the contractor. Phase Two testing on performance and handling characteristics began on 24 August 1948 and was completed on 9 December 1948. Twenty-two flights were made with a total of 31 hours and 35 minutes flight time. A series of stability and control tests were begun on 31

March 1949. These tests were terminated on 11 July 1949 before their completion.

The tests revealed that the XB-48 did not meet the guarantees; however, top speed at 35,000 ft was the only item in which the aircraft fell considerable short. The guarantee was 536 mph at 35,000 ft, but the actual speed was 479 mph. Its top speed turned out to be 516 mph at 20,000 ft. The flight tests also revealed other deficiencies: too sensitive nose gear

Above, ship one during Phase Two testing. (NARA via Bill Spidle)

steering, excessive turbulence in the bomb bay when open, insufficent lateral trim at high speeds, and the hydraulic system chattered.

Also in July 1949, Martin was notified that ship one was no longer needed and that it would be used for spare parts and then scrapped.

MARTIN XB-48 SHIP TWO, S/N 45-59586

There were a number of differences between ship one and the more refined ship two. Ship two, S/N 45-59586, had a fully functional bomb bay, a dummy version of the Emerson B-45 twin .50 cal remote control tail turret, an electric blanket anti-icing system and the improved J35-9 engines with I-40 fuel control systems.

Ship two was cleared for ground testing on 9 July 1948. Ground testing and vibration tests were completed by 1 August 1948 and by 11 August electrical, starter systems and outrigger gear stress tests were finished. Ship two began taxi tests on 13 August. First flight had been scheduled for 17 September 1948 but was delayed a month due to lack of GFE equipment and the rework of exhaust

pipes and aft landing gear. The above rework was completed by 15 October 1948 and the missing GFE equipment was waived for the first flight. The waved items were: anti-icing wind-

Below, ship two, S/N 45-59586, at Martin on 20 July 1948. Note missing fin cap and lack of nose markings. (NARA via Bill Spidle)

At top, ship two on 24 July 1948. Note dummy Emerson B-45 type tail turret and missing fin tip. (GLMMAM Archive) Above, ship two during taxi tests on 1 February 1949. (GLMMAM Archive) Below, prepping for an engine start on ship two in October 1948. Note "The Middle River Stump Jumper" at right. (GLMMAM Archive)

shield panel, fuel gage dials, and anti-icing blankets.

The 30-minute first flight to NAS Patuxent River, MD, was conducted on 16 October 1948. The aircraft was returned to Martin for the installation of the missing GFE equipment on 25 October after which flight testing was completed in November and the acceptance inspection was held from 5 to 7 January 1949. Final acceptance was made at Martin's plant on 23 February 1949.

The airplane was delivered to Wright Field in March 1949. The Bombardment Branch requested that all laboratories submit a list of tests they wished to accomplish because no production order was being considered. The proposed program as of June 1949 was to test anti-icing systems and to check out pilots on landing heavy multi-jet aircraft equiped with bicycle gear. The anti-icing tests were completed in mid-1951 and the aircraft was ferried to Phillips Field, Aberdeen Proving Grounds, MD, where it was structure tested until it was destroyed.

This page, ship two first flight taxi and take-off on 16 October 1948. (GLM-MAM Archive)